Your Kingdom Come
Living out the Lord's Prayer

Michael Sullivant

CREATION
HOUSE

YOUR KINGDOM COME by Michael Sullivant
Published by Creation House
A part of Strang Communications Company
600 Rinehart Road
Lake Mary, Florida 32746
www.creationhouse.com

Unless otherwise noted, all Scripture quotations are from the New King James Version of the Bible. Copyright © 1979, 1980, 1982 by Thomas Nelson, Inc., publishers. Used by permission.

Scripture quotations marked KJV are from the King James Version of the Bible.

Scripture quotations marked NAS are from the New American Standard Bible. Copyright © 1960, 1962, 1963, 1968, 1971, 1972, 1973, 1975, 1977 by the Lockman Foundation. Used by permission. (www.Lockman.org)

Scripture quotations marked NIV are from the Holy Bible, New International Version. Copyright © 1973, 1978, 1984, International Bible Society. Used by permission.

Scripture quotations marked TLB are from The Living Bible. Copyright © 1971. Used by permission of Tyndale House Publishers, Inc., Wheaton, IL 60189. All rights reserved.

All song lyrics are from *Your Kingdom Come* by Craig Smith, copyright © 2000 Integrity's Allelulia! Music/SESAC. All rights reserved. Used by permission.

Library of Congress Catalog Card Number: 00-105505
International Standard Book Number: 0-88419-690-9

0 1 2 3 4 5 6 7 VERSA 8 7 6 5 4 3 2 1
Printed in the United States of America

Contents

Jesus Christ personally gave the Lord's Prayer to all humanity in direct response to His disciples' passionate appeal to Him: "Lord, teach us to pray" (Luke 11:1). This prayer has become, by far, the most famous and often repeated biblical prayer in world history. Contained within it is an unchanging and yet ever unfolding ingenious pattern of themes that is able to usher the soul of the spiritual seeker into a vital connection with the divine. In it, we have a theologically profound, historically proven and spiritually potent resource.

Music is a heavenly creation given to the earth. It penetrates the human soul with an efficiency that words alone cannot achieve. For many—including the present generation—music is the universal language that crosses cultural, generational and language barriers. The psalmists of the Bible understood this amazing power and put their inspired prayers to music. The prophets would sometimes call the minstrels to help set the stage for the manifestation of God's presence and power.

> "But now bring me a musician." Then it happened, when the musician played, that the hand of the LORD came upon him [Elisha].
>
> —2 KINGS 3:15

Music is something that occupies the angelic hosts themselves. The history of the universal Church is filled with testimony of how prayer warriors have utilized music to inspire and assist them in their holy preoccupation of worship and intercession.

Like the four living creatures, we are invited to lift up to God both the "harp" (musical worship) and the "bowl" (verbal intercession) with the Holy Spirit's help.

> Now when He had taken the scroll, the four living creatures and the twenty-four elders fell down before the Lamb, each having a harp, and golden bowls full of incense, which are the prayers of the saints.
>
> —REVELATION 5:8

I believe that the combining and mingling of music and prayer within the hearts and upon the lips of believers in Christ will truly help to deliver the Church from much of her spiritual boredom in the coming days.

It was in the light of these realities that Craig Smith received his inspiration to write and record a musical prayer project based around the Lord's Prayer. In the early part of 1999, Craig shared his vision with me while we were ministering together in Winnipeg, Canada. We began to imagine together the spiritual potential of multiplied thousands of Christians memorizing, internalizing, verbalizing and singing the awesome themes of this great prayer over and over again and then passing the songs—and the truths they contain—on to their children and grandchildren. Ancient strongholds of evil could be shaken from their places as the hearts and minds of such worshipers would be drawn into and encamped around God's mighty throne of grace and beauty. Many Christians would be empowered to storm the gates of hell by the glorious means of storming the throne of God with musically animated love, devotion and intercession that surely would not be denied powerful divine responses. It might become a catalyst for a divine "ambush"—first for human hearts and then for the evil satanic powers hovering over and working within the nations.

During that time Craig and I talked and prayed together about the possibility of my authoring an accompanying devotional book as a part of the project. The book would serve as a user-friendly, interactive devotional tool that would be interfaced with the themes of the Lord's Prayer and make references to the lyrics of the songs on the recording. It would seek to expose and elaborate upon some of the life-changing truths implied by the prayer and also draw the readers into actually responding in prayer as they read. We felt that this book would need to stand on its own as an individual work, but that it could also be used as a follow-up tool for individuals and groups who would be impacted by Craig's songs. It might serve to take those who got "caught" by the music into a deeper contemplation of the Lord's Prayer and its transforming power. I immediately came home from that trip, wrote the first draft of this book and sent it to Craig. I hoped to spark him with ideas and language for some of his song lyrics.

Since then, we have been amazed and filled with gratitude as we have watched the Holy Spirit breathe on the project from its initial starting point. He brought our friends— experts in different industries—together from around the country to make our vision a living reality. We are thankful for Paul Mills, Craig's longtime friend and the producer of the recording; the great musicians who played and sang so skillfully for the glory of God; Chris Thomason, the head of the creative department for Integrity Music; Rick Nash, director of product development at Creation House, and Barbara Dycus, my editor. We are also especially thankful for our precious wives, Dianna Smith and Terri Sullivant, who have stood with us through the many years of marriage and ministry in ways too numerous to recount. Craig and I both know that we could not have served the body of Christ with a project like this without their support and faithfulness to both God and us.

If this book touches your heart and you haven't yet purchased the Integrity Music recording *Your Kingdom Come* by Craig Smith, I would encourage you to do so. You will be deeply moved by it. Throughout the book, I have included the stirring lyrics of Craig's songs. May the heavenly Father, the Lord Jesus Christ and the blessed Holy Spirit meet you mightily as you read, ponder, pray and listen!

—MICHAEL SULLIVANT
KANSAS CITY, MISSOURI

The Lord's Prayer

Our Father which art in heaven,
Hallowed be thy name.
Thy kingdom come.
Thy will be done
In earth, as it is in heaven.
Give us this day our daily bread.
And forgive us our debts,
As we forgive our debtors.
And lead us not into temptation,
But deliver us from evil:
For thine is the kingdom, and the power, and the glory, for
  ever. Amen.

—MATTHEW 6:9–13, KJV

Embracing the
Mystery of Prayer

Can an irresistible force create an immovable object?" Some agnostics use this saying as supposed "proof" that humans cannot really know if God exists. They ask this hypothetical question, and then sit back smugly, convinced they are safely "off the hook" in terms of their personal responsibility to relate to their Creator.

Such a statement can send the human mind into a paralyzing loop of contradictory and irresolvable thoughts. Agnostics conclude from that mind confusion, created by this statement as to the question of the existence of an all-powerful God, that obviously no one can really come to know the answer. These people believe by inventing this kind of mind game that they have set forth an airtight case for their position of nonbelief.

However, God, who is not under any pressure to validate His existence, remains unmoved—He is not impressed by such games.

Unfortunately, many people have overlooked the staggering reality that our Creator is so much more than an irresistible, impersonal "force." Indeed, He has infinite power, but it is governed by His very personal love for His creation. God is personal, and God is love. Moreover, God has purposefully chosen to "blow our [finite] minds" by the lofty truths about His nature and His ways. Strangely to some, this is one of His ways of alluring us to fall in love with Him. He knows how desperately we all need to connect personally with the One who is transcendentally majestic. Instinctively we long to interface with

1

Someone who is infinite and incomprehensible. In addition, we know instinctively that our Creator must have such attributes — and we are strangely comforted in our inability to fully grasp His majesty.

Our loving Creator, who is simultaneously transcendent and immanent, doesn't force Himself upon us. True love is voluntary by nature. God is playing hide-and-seek with humanity, only it's not a game. It is a sober reality. Parents play peekaboo and hide-and-seek with their children purposely to create the exciting tension of the possibility of losing the loved one. Thus the thrill and joy of the love between parent and child will be felt all over again and again and not taken for granted.

All of human history — the agony and ecstasy of the rising and falling of nations, the periodic shifting of their national boundaries and our very purpose on this planet — revolves around God's will that we should seek after Him. He has ordained for our good not only the finding of Himself, but also the groping after Him itself (Acts 17:24–27). The *journey* is as necessary as the *destination* for our personal growth.

By strategically placing mystery and paradox at the heart of a life of faith, God protects us from our destructive arrogance. Although the natural human mind is often offended in God's economy, He has designed our spirits to thrive on being touched by and rising to touch His mysteries. Western Christianity has done much to "sterilize" the gospel of Jesus Christ. This is due to the prevalent rationalism that has spread to our culture through our educational institutions, which have been steeped in the doctrines of the "Enlightenment." This European movement of the eighteenth century was a revival of pre-Christian Greek culture and philosophy. Under the cultural pressure to be more modern and intellectual, many Christians and Christian leaders have become too apologetic about the mystery of our faith rather than simply holding it forth and proclaiming it to humanity.

Ironically, our present generation is actually hungry for mystery. The Church is privy to the greatest mysteries of the universe—the Trinity, the manifest presence of God, prophecy, the Incarnation, the cross, the Resurrection, the new birth and prayer itself. Many Christians have foolishly overlooked one of our greatest evangelistic tools in order to appease the shifting and fickle spirit of the world!

Mystery "messes" with us in a good way. It reminds us that God is the center of the universe, not we. Its presence is intended to lead us into humility, worship and passionate service before His Majesty. The mystery of God places and keeps us in our proper place in this universe and positions us to fulfill our marvelous destiny as His children.

The reality of prayer is truly an amazing phenomenon ordained by an all-wise God. Because of our natural thinking, it is hard for us to receive the lofty and magnificent promises regarding prayer in Holy Scripture. Because of our hardened hearts, it is easy for us to underestimate the power of God that is available to us through prayer. Because of our obvious finiteness, it is easy for us to doubt and question our ability to influence and affect our infinite Creator, His intentions and His actions by appealing to Him with our weak words. These are difficult things for us to grasp, and they are literally impossible for us to grasp with our natural minds. It takes the revelation of the Holy Spirit to convince us of such a truth as Christian prayer.

> But as it is written: "Eye has not seen, nor ear heard, nor have entered into the heart of man the things which God has prepared for those who love Him." But God has revealed them to us through His Spirit. For the Spirit searches all things, yes, the deep things of God. . . . Now we have received, not the spirit of the world, but the Spirit who is from God, that we might know the things that have been freely given to us by God. . . . But the natural man does not receive the things of the Spirit of God, for they are foolishness to him; nor can he know them, because they are spiritually discerned.
>
> —1 CORINTHIANS 2:9–10, 12, 14

Prayer, above and beyond many other things, is one of these "things of the Spirit of God."

DANCING WITH THE DIVINE: DIVINE INITIATIVE, HUMAN RESPONSE AND DIVINE RESPONSE TO HUMAN RESPONSE

Ironically, we are afraid of the very thing for which we most deeply long and for which we are most essentially designed — a genuine interactive relationship with our awesome Creator. Can you see this reflected in the application of the scripture below?

> Then He said to them, "Take heed what you hear. With the same measure you use [in response to God], it will be measured [back] to you [by God]; and to you who hear [and respond], more will be given [in response from God]."
> —MARK 4:24

There is a general pattern in Scripture that addresses the way that God interacts with humanity. The first movement is *God's movement toward us*. This speaks of the fundamental place of grace in our relationship with God. God is a God who has always issued invitations to people to come into a relationship with Him.

> Ho! Everyone who thirsts, come to the waters; and you who have no money, come, buy and eat. Yes, come, buy wine and milk without money and without price. Why do you spend money for what is not bread, and your wages for what does not satisfy? Listen carefully to Me, and eat what is good, and let your soul delight itself in abundance.
>
> Incline your ear, and come to Me. Hear, and your soul shall live; and I will make an everlasting covenant with you — the sure mercies of David.
> —ISAIAH 55:1–3

Without this kind of unmerited invitation there would be no basis for our relating to God.

The second movement is also vital in God's plan. It deals with *human response to these divine invitations*. It is as though

God is passionately looking for a proper and faithful response on our part to His gracious initiatives.

> For the eyes of the LORD run to and fro throughout the whole earth, to show Himself strong on behalf of those whose heart is loyal to Him.
>
> —2 CHRONICLES 16:9

The third movement relates to the *divine response to human response*. This third movement in the dance between the divine and human has often been neglected, yet it is absolutely necessary for creating an accurate picture of the interactive relationship.

In the history of Christianity, some religious movements have emphasized the first movement in a way that has de-emphasized the second movement. This has often inadvertently led to a kind of *fatalism* among professing Christians. An example of this would be groups that have gotten into an extreme form of predestination.

Other religious movements have emphasized the second movement in such a way that the first movement has been improperly de-emphasized or even overlooked. This has inadvertently led to *legalism* among professing Christians. An example of this would be groups that have gotten into an extreme form of human freedom. Many times these groups that have fallen into both extremes have virtually neglected the third movement altogether. This has led to a spiritual sterility that can best be described as a *boring* form of Christianity!

This is not a new problem among professed believers. In the first century the apostle Paul made it clear that people who were associated with the Church had fallen into a watered-down form of faith.

> . . . having a form of godliness but denying its power.
>
> —2 TIMOTHY 3:5

I believe that the inclusion of this third movement—*divine response to human response*—is a major key to the experience of a *passionate* and *wholehearted* interactive relationship with

God. We must be grounded upon the firm foundation of the grace of God in our relationship to Him. Also, we must build upon this foundation by continually cultivating a faithful response to His divine initiatives. However, we must respond with a living hope that God will Himself respond to our responses. *The inclusion of the third movement of this marvelous dance between God and us is vital for the proper motivation of a healthy life of prayer.*

Although God dwells in infinity and eternity, He condescends to relate genuinely to us in time and space—here and now. Solomon understood profoundly and referred to these two realities in a single prayer:

> But will God indeed dwell on the earth? Behold, heaven and the heaven of heavens cannot contain You. How much less this temple which I have built! [Solomon knew God was transcendent and omnipresent.]
>
> Yet regard the prayer of Your servant and his supplication, O LORD my God, and listen to the cry and the prayer which Your servant is praying before You today. [Solomon also knew God's passion to visit with humanity here and now in time and space and to reveal His manifest presence.]
>
> —1 KINGS 8:27–28

Isaiah echoes this same truth.

> For thus says the high and exalted One who lives forever, whose name is Holy, "I dwell on a high and holy place [God's transcendence], and also with the contrite and lowly of spirit in order to revive the spirit of the lowly and to revive the heart of the contrite" [God's immanence].
>
> —ISAIAH 57:15, NAS

Many people are paralyzed in their interaction with God because they are psychologically and emotionally overwhelmed with the concept of His infinitude and the keen awareness of their human weaknesses and limitations.

However, the Bible teaches us over and over again that *our humanity does not automatically hinder us from enjoying a personal friendship with God.* In fact, human life has been designed to interface with God's life. The Scriptures teach us about the passion in God's heart to have such a vital relationship with us and to confer upon us His awesome delegated authority. King David also marveled at this divine arrangement between God and humans.

> When I consider Your heavens, the work of Your fingers,
> The moon and the stars, which You have ordained,
> What is man that You are mindful of him,
> And the son of man that You visit him?
> For You have made him a little lower than the angels,
> And You have crowned him with glory and honor.
> You have made him to have dominion over the works
>   of Your hands;
> You have put all things under His feet.
>
> —PSALM 8:3–6

When the apostle James writes to us about the powerful praying and prophetic ministry of Elijah, his practical point is not that Elijah is in a category of humanity different from our own. Rather, it is the exact opposite. His point is that if Elijah could relate to God this way, then the potential is present for us to do the same.

> Confess your trespasses to one another, and pray for one another, that you may be healed. The effective, fervent prayer of a righteous man avails much. *Elijah was a man with a nature like ours,* and he prayed earnestly that it would not rain; and it did not rain on the land for three years and six months. And he prayed again, and the heaven gave rain, and the earth produced its fruit.
>
> —JAMES 5:16–18, EMPHASIS ADDED

James does not use the example of Elijah to "put stars in our eyes" by seeing how awesome the prophet of God was, but to

7

motivate us to pray to the very same awesome God of the prophets! God will listen to our voice also.

THE KINGDOM OF GOD IS A "DOUBLE FEATURE"

In a spiritual dream, I saw the kingdom of God as having two theaters operating concurrently. The first theater represented God's sovereign activity in relation to His purposes. The second theater represented the arena of human responsibility as it relates to God's purposes. It was like a double feature, only the "shows" were playing at the same time. This was a word play on "two features" of God's kingdom purposes—*God's part* and *our part*. This could also represent two general "features," or aspects, of God's ways with humanity.

I saw many people milling around the first theater, trying to peer into the deep mysteries that surround divine sovereignty. They were captivated by the intrigue that it involves. However, the second theater was almost empty. This was an urgent concern on the Lord's heart. Many of God's people were so fascinated by the first theater that they were neglecting their arena of responsibility. Their carnal inquisitiveness was paralyzing them from taking action. In this particular scenario, their "philosophizing" was a subtle fleshly substitute for obeying!

I knew that the Lord wanted to shift His people's attention to the second theater and to draw them into it. The show that was playing there was not as intellectually intoxicating. It was very simple and practical. There was a posture of heart that was required to properly participate in this arena. It involved being in awe of the mystery of God's sovereignty (the show playing in the first theater) and allowing this reality to lead them into humility, prayer and worship (the show playing in the second theater). The mysteries of God will never be exhausted by our finite minds. God has strategically ordained this dynamic.

In the next scene I saw the Lord as a general contractor of a vast building project. He had hired us as subcontractors on the project. The subcontractors weren't to concern themselves with trying to do, or even to comprehend, the job of the general contractor—this would distract them from doing their part. They needed to focus on their jobs. The Lord didn't want people trying to occupy His "office." It is God's exclusive realm of responsibility to comprehend and righteously engineer the big picture of earthly activities in such a way that His name is glorified in the end. God is able even to turn evil upon its head to serve His ultimate purposes.

> Surely the wrath of man shall praise You; with the remainder of wrath You shall gird Yourself.
>
> —PSALM 76:10

In the last scene of the dream, I saw the sovereignty of God as a "safety net" under some acrobats. I knew that we were like those acrobats who, if they concentrated upon the net's presence, would be unable to perform their feats. They would miss their timing, their cues and their leaps and catches. God has called us to do kingdom exploits that require much preparation, self-discipline, timing, coordination, teamwork, courage, trust and skill. We should be truly grateful for the "safety net" of His mysterious sovereignty, but we should not allow its reality to distract us from the responsibilities before us. We are being called to do our part in the enterprise of God's kingdom. *We are saved by faith alone, but the faith that saves us is not alone.* Faith without works equals false faith and dead religion.

> For as the body without the spirit is dead, so faith without works is dead also.
>
> —JAMES 2:26

Through faith *we* must intercede, fast, humble ourselves, give generously, study, meditate, remember the poor, love our spouses and children, go to the unreached peoples, minister to the sick, evangelize the lost, serve our local church, preach and teach the Word of God, disciple new converts and develop a rich, secret devotional life. God will not do these things for us. *We cannot do the things that only God can do, and God will not do for us what*

Your Kingdom Come

He has called and empowered us to do with the promised help of the Holy Spirit.

> The secret things belong to the LORD our God, but those things which are revealed belong to us and to our children forever, that we may do all the words of this law.
> —DEUTERONOMY 29:29

We tend to be motivated, through both our carnality and the forces of modern culture, by what is novel. However, the things that God has ordained for us to do, although we may find fresh expressions for them, are simple, reasonable and historically established activities—activities like prayer.

May God help us to find our way back to the joyful labor and profound practice of "calling down" the power of His Spirit and kingdom, both night and day, upon the regions of this earth in the name of Jesus Christ our Lord. May we be enabled by Him to live out the other aspects of our lives in such a way that they become totally supportive of and integrated with this holy preoccupation of prayer. There is a way of making the many methods and forms of prayer a way of life—*our lives can actually "become" prayer.* David alludes to this kind of spiritual intensity in the following psalm.

> In return for my love they are my accusers, but *I prayer.*
> —PSALM 109:4, LITERAL

LEARNING TO PRAY

The disciples undoubtedly discerned the gap between their experience with prayer and Jesus' experience. The Gospel of Luke states that on one occasion after Jesus finished praying, one of His disciples said (obviously inquiring not only for his sake, but also for the sake of the other disciples as well), "Lord, teach us to pray, as John also taught his disciples" (Luke 11:1). In response to this request, Jesus taught them what has come to be known as "the Lord's Prayer." The wisdom of the Scriptures states, "We do not know how to pray as we should" (Rom. 8:26, NAS). The Holy Spirit, however, who knows well how to pray according to the will of God, is committed to helping us in our weakness.

The disciples' request in Luke exemplifies the first two qualifications for entering a life of prayer. First, we must admit our ignorance and weakness. Second, we must rely on Someone beyond ourselves, although living and moving within us, to empower and teach us. This is none other than the Holy Spirit Himself, who inhabits all believers in Christ.

Given that the Holy Spirit is the Author of the Scriptures, what better place could there be to find the raw material the Spirit uses as He teaches us to pray? And what better prayer recorded in Scripture could we turn to than the very one in which Jesus specifically instructs us how to pray? We will be exploring this inspired prayer phrase by phrase in the following sections of this book. Before we do this, let's take a broader look at the prayer in its context.

> And when you pray, you shall not be like the hypocrites. For they love to pray standing in the synagogues and on the corners of the streets, that they may be seen by men. Assuredly, I say to you, they have their reward. But you, when you pray, go into your room, and when you have shut your door, pray to your Father who is in the secret place; and your Father who sees in secret will reward you openly. And when you pray, do not use vain repetitions as the heathen do. For they think that they will be heard for their many words. Therefore do not be like them. For your Father knows the things you have need of before you ask Him.
>
> —MATTHEW 6:5–8

From Jesus' teaching on prayer in this passage, we can draw a few general principles:

- Acceptable prayer depends on the motivations of the heart in God's sight, in contrast with the outward form of prayer in the sight of others.

11

- Acceptable prayer is simple and straightforward, not complicated or unattainable.

- Acceptable prayer does not inform God of anything, but instead forms us spiritually. Prayer produces enormous changes, especially in us.

TWENTY-ONE PRAYERFACTS THAT HELP TO REMOVE OBSTACLES TO A LIFE OF PRAYER

And it shall be said, "Build up, build up, prepare the way, remove every obstacle out of the way of My people."
—ISAIAH 57:14, NAS

One way of defining the best kind of human life is to regard it as a life of prayer. God has actually designed us for fellowship and communion with Him—we are built for God. The idea that the invisible, eternal, omnipotent, omniscient and omnipresent Creator would be pleased to ordain such things as truly listening and responding to finite and fallen creatures is an amazing concept. Yet, as we come to understand the nature of God, the nature of love and the purpose of human existence, it is reasonable to think that God, in His wisdom, would do so. Many powerful forces, both within ourselves and from beyond us, are bent on hindering us from knowing the truth about prayer—and especially bent on hindering us from actually praying.

Ironically, after some simple basics are understood, the best way of learning about prayer is simply to practice it—personally and corporately. However, in order to combat the natural and supernatural forces that militate against such a life, we need a solid basis of conviction about the absolute necessity of a life of prayer. Ultimately, in order to live a life of prayer, we must get the revelational "root in ourselves" concerning the high and mysterious calling to intercession.

These likewise are the ones sown on stony ground who, when they hear the word, immediately receive it with gladness; and they have no root in themselves, and so endure

only for a time. Afterward, when tribulation or persecution
arises for the word's sake, immediately they stumble.
—MARK 4:16–17

Throughout the chapters of this book are interspersed a
series of connected prayerfacts that spiral upward and become
the basis of a psychologically sound (thoroughly and inter-
nally processed and resolved) way of being progressively led
into a life of prayer. Our prayer life must be based on a living
understanding lest it become a passionless, mechanical and
ineffective duty rather than a genuine, vibrant and conversa-
tional relationship with our God. We need to locate and trace
the fundamental biblical truths that will actually inspire us to
commit ourselves to a life of prayer.

We often fail to pray because we don't believe in the reality
of prayer on the psychological, emotional and, oftentimes,
philosophical/theological level. If we truly were deeply convinced of the loving connection we have with God and that He
offers us a constant audience with Him, we would pray much
more freely and often.

Use the prayerfacts throughout this book to aid in removing
any obstacles that are keeping you from living a life of prayer.

OUTLINE OF THE LORD'S PRAYER

Turning now to the main elements of the Lord's Prayer, we see
the following progression:

Worship—Our Father in heaven, hallowed be Your name.
Intercession—Your kingdom come. Your will be done
on earth as it is in heaven.
Personal petition—Give us this day our daily bread.
Confession of sin—And forgive us our debts,
Forgiveness of others—As we forgive our debtors.
Guidance—And do not lead us into temptation,
Warfare—But deliver us from the evil one.
Bold declaration—For Yours is the kingdom and the
power and the glory forever. Amen.

Your Kingdom Come

As helpful as it has been through the centuries, isn't it likely that Jesus was giving us much more than a few lines of prayer to memorize so we could recite them at church services and before bed? Long ago it was said that all other prayers are embedded in this one. Could this model prayer be a "table of contents" to a whole "book," with each phrase potentially representing a general category that contains a vast number of possible things to say to God that touch His heart? This book assumes that the latter is indeed true. I pray that as you read on, you will experience the deep truths behind the simple language of the most famous prayer the world has ever known.

> *Father in heaven, I pray that You would open to me the secrets of powerful prayer waiting to be discovered and explored in this all too familiar prayer. I confess that I do not know how to pray very well. As I contemplate the marvelous themes of the Lord's Prayer, come, Holy Spirit, and personally teach me and guide me to connect more deeply with the Father and the Son. Amen.*

One

"Our Father"

Prayer Element—Worship

Father

BRIDGE
Our Father who art in heaven
Hallowed be Thy name
Our Father who art in heaven
Hallowed be Thy name

VERSE
Father Heavenly Father
There is no one like You
Father Eternal Father
We bow our hearts before You
Father of lights our hope our future
We rest securely in You

CHORUS
Father You are Lord of the heavens
You are Lord of the earth
Father You are God in the highest
You are God of all life
Forever our Father
You are

No love is higher than Your love
You call us the children of God
Father protector provider
Our lives are destined in you
You carefully nurture
The lives of Your children
Safe in Your arms we abide

(Repeat chorus)

You are the Holy Righteous One
Faithful
Father
God

In this first phrase of the Lord's Prayer, Jesus invites His followers to pray and to worship the very same eternal and all-powerful Person to whom He prayed and from whom He drew His strength. As God the Son, Jesus Christ holds the unique position of Son of God. Yet He also identifies His students and followers as "sons and daughters" of God Almighty, for we are invited to address God as our Father. Jesus did not jealously guard His direct access to God, but He generously opened the way for us to enjoy an intimate relationship with the Father. After His resurrection He told Mary Magdalene, "I am ascending to My Father and your Father, and to My God and your God" (John 20:17).

FACING OUR DEEP LONELINESS

As we are born into this fallen world, a deep sense of loneliness screams silently from within the human spirit. Neither I nor anyone else on earth knows the depths of my being in the way I long to be known. No one loves me the way I long to be loved, not even the kindest mother or the most faithful spouse. Amid the teaming masses of people and things in this world, I am yet lonely. In reality, I am lonely for the God who alone knows and loves me perfectly.

Yet, He has made Himself invisible, and I am afraid that He won't really be there for me if I try somehow to seek for and connect with Him. In the fear and frustration of my loneliness, I am tempted to strike out on my own to try to find something—anything—more concrete to soothe the ache and the groan of my spirit. Like others all around me, I have sought to fill the hollow vacuum of my heart with human loves and relationships, entertainment, recreations, achievements, labors, learning, possessions, distractions, earthly pleasures (that so easily become addictions) and a myriad of other "commodities" on the "market" in this world's grand "exhibition hall." Still, I painfully learn again and again that all these, as good as some of them are

> ## PRAYERFACT 1
>
> *God our Creator has given human beings a measure of self-subsistent power called natural life.*
>
> —Prayerfact 2 (see page 29)

in their proper place, do not satisfy my deepest longings. My spirit persistently informs me that *I am built for God*, my Creator. As the great French philosopher and mathematician Pascal noted, there is a "God-shaped void" in the human heart.

Amazingly, in the Bible we discover that not only are we lonely for God, but He is, in a sense, "lonely" for us. God wants us to want Him, and He also intensely wants us. Not only are we in need of having the void filled by God, but God is passionate to fill the void and live within us. God is earnestly desirous of having a loving friendship and genuine partnership with human beings. His heart has been yearning for us from the very beginning. This is why He sent His only begotten Son to seek us out and to make a way to restore our relationship with Him.

> For the Son of Man has come to seek and to save that which was lost.
>
> —LUKE 19:10

The original sin and guilt of our first parents, passed down to all of us through the generations by natural birth, created a barrier between us and our Creator. But Christ came to smash through this barrier and to reconnect us to the One who made us, knows us and loves us. He came to reconcile us to God—His Father and our Father.

> For God so loved the world that He gave His only begotten Son, that whoever believes in Him should not perish but have everlasting life. For God did not send His Son

into the world to condemn the world, but that the world
through Him might be saved.

—JOHN 3:16–17

It's mind-boggling to consider that the almighty and infinite
God, who can live wherever He pleases, has desired literally to
dwell within human beings. In Christ, we individually—
including our very physical body—become a *temple* of God.

> Or do you not know that your body is the temple of the
> Holy Spirit who is in you, whom you have from God, and
> you are not your own?
>
> —1 CORINTHIANS 6:19

This means that the Father, Son and Holy Spirit live, move
and have Their being within you! It's useless to ask *how* this
is possible, or even *why* He has chosen to arrange it this way.
It's supposed to stun us and overwhelm us to the point that we
simply embrace it, enjoy it and live it out.

> For you are the temple of the living God. As God has
> said: "I will dwell in them and walk among them. I will
> be their God, and they shall be My people. . . . I will be a
> Father to you, and you shall be My sons and daughters,
> says the LORD Almighty."
>
> —2 CORINTHIANS 6:16, 18

AN INTIMATE CONNECTION WITH GOD

In this work of salvation, Jesus dealt with the guilt and shame
of the sins of all humanity. He did this by offering Himself as
the substitutionary sacrifice for each one of us. The justice of
God demanded a death penalty for sin—for "the wages of sin"
have always been "death" in one form or another (Rom. 6:23).
Only "God in the flesh" could have proven to be such a worthy sacrifice. Only a "son of man" could have represented all
humanity before God. Jesus Christ is that eternally unique
God/man. God Himself, in Christ, suffered for us, shed His
blood for us and died for us on a cruel cross. On the third day

after His death, He was raised back to life by the power of the Holy Spirit. Thus the way was opened for human beings literally to receive new life by placing their faith and trust in Jesus Christ.

> Moreover, brethren, I declare to you the gospel which I preached to you, which also you received and in which you stand, by which also you are saved, if you hold fast that word which I preached to you—unless you believed in vain. For I delivered to you first of all that which I also received: that Christ died for our sins according to the Scriptures, and that He was buried, and that He rose again the third day according to the Scriptures.
>
> —1 CORINTHIANS 15:1–4

The passionate love God has in His great heart for us was forever demonstrated through the death and resurrection of Christ. Now He can receive many *children* into the wonder of knowing Him, not only as our *Creator*, but also as our *Father*. As believers in Christ, we belong to God both by creation and by redemption. We are genuinely reconnected to and united with God our Maker.

Christ, so unlike us in His eternal deity, humbled Himself to become like us in order to reach down and lift us up to become like He is—not to deify us, but to exalt us in our divinely glorified humanity. *For He now is, and will forever be, a glorified human being—a fact that many Christians fail to grasp.* This is a profound commentary on the essential beauty and dignity that God has conferred upon the human race. As amazing as it sometimes seems to be, God really does love, and like, people.

All people are born with a longing and a need for *intimacy*—a kind of relational connectedness in which we are known fully by another and know that other fully. Yet there is no experience of *rejection* in the relationship. As we set out in life, we sooner or later painfully discover that no earthly relationship can touch the depth of this longing. This longing is an eternal heart-cry to touch and be touched by our Creator. Only

He can ultimately satisfy the deepest need we have for intimacy. This is a God-designed hunger and thirst that He has planted within our souls, hopefully to work to set us on the journey of seeking after God.

When we come to faith in Jesus Christ, the Holy Spirit comes to reside within us. As He does, we tap into the true source of intimacy—the Fatherhood of God over our lives.

> And because you are sons, God has sent forth the Spirit
> of His Son into your hearts, crying out, "Abba, Father!"
> —GALATIANS 4:6

Abba is the equivalent of "Daddy" or "Papa." Through Christ, God becomes our dear daddy. This is truly astounding, and it has rocked and will forever rock the religions of the world. The awesome Creator is accessible to us on the terms of a very deep intimacy. When I connect with God in this way and address Him as my "Papa," the vacuum of loneliness begins to be filled with the knowledge of His acceptance and care over my life. My "Papa" is on the scene of my life, and He can and will absorb my pain, my shame and my failures. He will empower me by His love and faith in me to reenter my world with restored, yet properly humbled, confidence.

The presence of the Holy Spirit in our souls also significantly speaks and ministers to the deep loneliness that we have known in our years of separation from the divine.

> And I will pray the Father, and He will give you another
> Helper, that He may abide with you forever—the Spirit
> of truth, whom the world cannot receive, because it nei-
> ther sees Him nor knows Him; but you know Him, for He
> dwells with you and will be in you. I will not leave you
> orphans; I will come to you. A little while longer and the
> world will see Me no more, but you will see Me. Because
> I live, you will live also. At that day you will know that I
> am in My Father, and you in Me, and I in you.
> —JOHN 14:16–20

Your Kingdom Come

Note that despite our deepening experience of having intimacy with God, the groan of our loneliness will not be fully removed in this earthly life. No matter how closely we relate to God in this life, we will yet long to see Him face to face. Real intimacy with God is available to us now, but full intimacy with God awaits our departure from this world or the return of Christ, whichever comes first. In fact, ironically, the more acquainted we become with God, the more intensely we will long to depart and be with Him. We taste enough of the pleasure of divine friendship here and now that our souls are branded and forever after are conscious that our true homeland, our destination, is not in this fallen age.

God uses this dynamic tension of tasting real intimacy with God and not yet enjoying full intimacy with God to keep us longing in a healthy way for the eternal age to come. Moreover, far from leading us into an irresponsible way of life on earth, this experience gives us our proper bearings for living the best earthly lives possible. Remember that the purpose of an effective appetizer is not to satisfy our appetite, but to stimulate our hunger for the full meal to come. It is not that we become "so heavenly minded that we're no earthly good," but that we become "so heavenly minded" that we actually become some "earthly good." Heavenly minded people make the best earthly citizens, for they bear the very presence of God into a fallen world and hold out to all others the hope and message of humanity's salvation in Jesus Christ.

> For we know that the whole creation groans and labors with birth pangs together until now. Not only that, but we also who have the firstfruits of the Spirit, even we ourselves groan within ourselves, eagerly waiting for the adoption, the redemption of our body. For we were saved in this hope, but hope that is seen is not hope; for why does one still hope for what he sees? But if we hope for what we do not see, we eagerly wait for it with perseverance.
>
> —ROMANS 8:22–25

Don't receive the claims of religions, philosophies or those peddling the plethora of spiritual or earthly experiences or regimens that guarantee, in one way or another, that you can get rid of the "groan" of Romans 8:23. This groan has been designed by God to keep us from settling down in a wrong way in this fallen world. We must brace ourselves and be reconciled to its presence from the outset of our journey in Christ.

> For here we have no continuing city, but we seek the one
> to come.
>
> —HEBREWS 13:14

OUR SOURCE OF IDENTITY

Who are we really? We all long deeply to know the real answer. Of course, we do have a name by which we are identified. But a name is a label that metaphorically represents much more than at first meets the eye or ear. Interestingly enough, we didn't choose for ourselves this tag that so marks our existence in the world. This speaks of the undeniable influence upon us by our parents and our ancestors that were before them. We didn't come into this world in isolation from others, and neither do we live our lives in isolation from others. We are profoundly connected both to past generations and to people in our lives today. This fact should humble us.

Maybe if we look more deeply into the meaning behind our being *named*, we will gain deeper insight into our true identity. The apostle Paul said that God's whole family in heaven and earth derives its name from the Father of our Lord Jesus Christ.

> For this reason I bow my knees to the Father of our Lord
> Jesus Christ, from whom the whole family in heaven and
> earth is named.
>
> —EPHESIANS 3:14–15

In other words, *the fatherhood of God* is the source of every believer's *true identity* in Christ. God has given us our most meaningful "name"—*daughters and sons of the living God.*

Just as natural fathers pass on their surnames to their children, so our heavenly Father has named Christians after Himself (James 2:7). This name is spoken over us and called down upon us in baptism (Matt. 28:19). From where and from whom have we come? Only by discovering these answers will we know where we are to go and whom we are to become. The only way we will come to know ourselves is by beginning with a reference point beyond ourselves. Of course, God Himself is the most stable and unchanging reference point that there could ever be.

> Every good gift and every perfect gift is from above, and comes down from the Father of lights, with whom there is no variation or shadow of turning.
>
> —JAMES 1:17

When we connect with God, we find the center of all things—thereby finding our own bearings for our lives and destinies. When we find God, we find the big X on the map of the universe that says "Begin Here." Knowing where we are in relation to God helps us to chart our course. God has provided the Scriptures to be that map, and He even sends His Spirit to be with us as a personal map reader and guide!

The most important thing about us is what we truly come to know about God! Knowing God is the key to living a fully human life, for we have been "wired" to interface with God and the powers of His heavenly kingdom. Our lives, our true identities, are *hidden* with Christ in God (Col. 3:3). We don't know who we are until we connect with our Creator. Through His Word and Spirit He informs us of who we are and what we are called to become.

This is not a one-time experience. Our "secret identity" in Christ is progressively revealed to us by God as we walk in friendship with Him—inviting Him into every arena of our life and loving, worshiping and serving Him throughout our years upon the earth. Even though we are already the children of God, it has not fully been revealed what we shall be. However, when He is revealed, we shall be like Him, for we shall see Him as He is (1 John 3:2). The Holy Spirit stamps the full image of God upon our hearts when we come to Christ. We are then progressively renewed in every aspect of our personalities according to that divine image. It is similar to the way a negative of a beautiful photograph, which is instantly imprinted on the film, must then be developed through a process into a clear and colorful picture that is worthy of admiration.

OUR SOURCE OF SECURITY

The heavenly Father is the source of our *security*. Just breathing out "Father" in prayer causes me instantly to feel safer and more protected in this world. Sadly, some people have never known love from their earthly fathers. They must first overcome the bad "father image" imprinted on their souls by the fathering failures of their dads before they can feel safe with God as Father. But the Holy Spirit will work to heal the broken "father image" in our hearts and will grant us a living revelation of our heavenly Father's truly perfect love and the greatness of His power. He will never leave us or forsake us.

We are not big enough, powerful enough or wise enough to protect ourselves effectively. Yet so often we still try to do so. But we don't have to. There is a Father in heaven who is up to the task. Too many of us waste our spiritual, emotional, physical and material energies trying to be our own god. However, the shoes of deity are just too big for us to fill. Just imagine the resources we will conserve when we learn to trust God more fully with our lives, our affairs and our futures. Loving fathers protect their little ones from harm. They provide for the needs of their little ones.

It is almost unimaginable that weak and sinful humans could become so free from fear and intimidation that we could have a warm and personal relationship with the infinite, all-powerful Creator of the universe. Yet this is exactly what Jesus has made available to us. Through Christ, God has become our Father. He is reigning securely upon the throne of the whole universe.

He sees and knows all things. He possesses the power to effect His will and fully defeat the forces of evil. He has promised ultimately to provide for all of our genuine needs. He has invited us to speak with Him at any time or in any place regarding the situations in our lives and the deepest feelings hidden in our hearts. This is the One who has loved us and who calls us to trust in Him. What greater security could be offered to us than what Christ has purchased for us with His life?

OUR SOURCE FOR PERSONAL GROWTH

A good father *trains and disciplines* his children to help form them into the quality of people he knows they can become. This molding and shaping is motivated from the love a father has for his offspring. He takes appropriate responsibility for their growth and development. Yet he also challenges them to accept their individual responsibility for their own growth. A good father does not *overprotect* his children. He encourages (i.e., "puts courage into") and empowers them to face the trials, pain and resistance that are necessary for their education. The heavenly Father is committed to using for good the pain that accompanies our living in a fallen world—the imperfect human relationships, the difficult circumstances and even the attacks of the devil. He works all these things together for our good to deepen the passion in our hearts for Him and His kingdom and to progressively perfect us by conforming us into the image of His Son Jesus (Rom. 8:29; 2 Cor. 3:18).

Pain and *passion* are philosophically linked. We call the week in which Christ died "Passion Week"—the week of His sufferings. *Compassion* is about "suffering with" others in their pain. We speak often these days about gaining and expressing *passion* for God and for Jesus in the body of Christ. However, we often don't realize that by this we are actually referring indirectly to our need to embrace not only the joyful blessings, but also the pain and suffering that God allows into our lives to shape and mold us by strategic pressure into the image of Christ. Ironically, without any pain there will be no passion. Pain is the crucible from which true spiritual passion is formulated.

When we encounter pain, we reconnect emotionally, from the heart, with the things that are most important in our life. These most important things relate to our need to love and be loved. But the kind of love of which the Bible speaks is always gutsy, costly and sacrificial in nature. These elements are what give love its value and substance. We all know this, but we tend to lose our focus upon it when the blessings of God are flowing our way. We like to imagine that we can enjoy meaningful and satisfying relationships without digging deep into our souls to the point that it hurts. Yet, we all know well the love we feel when others make painful and personal sacrifices for us. Why do we imagine that we can love well by some lesser means?

Our eternal joy in the age to come will be sweeter and richer because we have faced and overcome the pain of trials in this age. Without pain, we would too easily forget that "here we have no continuing city" (Heb. 13:14). Our healthy longing for the second appearing of Jesus and the age to come would be significantly dulled.

A true father is also a *leader* to his children. God is full of plans and purposes for His universe. He is guiding human history toward its determined goal—to sum everything up under the banner of Christ the Son. And God calls us forth into our purpose and function in this divine enterprise. It is His Fatherhood over us that first empowers us to rise up to be and to do. Our limited temporal purposes become caught up and intertwined with His

---

PRAYERFACT 2

—Prayerfact 1 (see page 20)

Although we cannot exist without the power of His providence operating in the universe, we can live a temporary earthly existence outside of believing in, loving and obeying Him.

—Prayerfact 3 (see page 42)

eternal purposes, and they take on a significance and meaning that human efforts and goals could never rise to on their own. By this, what He can potentially accomplish through us is astounding.

Another evidence of God's supreme leadership ability is that He does not chide us or mock us when we fail. He has tender mercy and pity upon us, for He knows that we are but dust and prone to trusting in our own strength. When we fail, God will often deal very gently with us. Usually before God will allow bad circumstances to result from our sin, the Holy Spirit will bring clear impressions to our minds and hearts that we are in the wrong. If we listen and respond, we can often avoid some of the negative fallout of our foolishness.

This is the nature of receiving *mercy* from God. Mercy is about God delivering us from the consequences of our sins. After David compromised his dignity and joined himself to fight with the Philistines, the mortal enemies of Israel, he wrote in Psalm 18:35: "Your gentleness has made me great." In this situation in David's life, God didn't harshly discipline him, for He knew of the hardships that David had unjustly suffered at the hand of jealous King Saul. It is often the kindness—rather than the punishment—of God that leads us to repentance in the midst of our temporary lapses into foolishness and compromise. Many times this divine kindness will melt our hardened hearts and woo us back into grateful obedience to God.

Even when we do come under the discipline of God, He still does not mock us for our failures. Rather, He disciplines us for our good to restore our souls and lead us deeper into His holiness. When we fail, God disciplines us to restore—not undermine—our personal dignity. This is why it is vital not to overreact in our flesh when God corrects us. At times people regard lightly the discipline of the Lord; at other times they faint under it. The Lord calls us simply to acknowledge our need for training in righteousness and not allow either fear or a paralyzing feeling of shame to distract us from the issue at hand. We must learn to anticipate gratefully and embrace the necessary and normal corrections that come with growing up in God. A good father deeply loves what he conceives. God knows and loves us (1 Cor. 8:3; Gal. 4:6–7). God actually possesses us (1 Cor. 6:19–20). God always corrects us out of His great love and concern for our best.

OUR SOURCE FOR COMMUNITY

Finally, the fact that God is our Father reminds us that we are born again in Christ into a spiritual *family*. He is *our* Father—the Father of our brothers and sisters as well as our own Father. Although genuine Christianity is very personal, it is not individualistic. A personal relationship with God is at the center of our faith, but it is not the circumference of it. This is why John could say that everyone who is born of God naturally loves his brother (1 John 4:7). The Church of Jesus is the community of God's people. We are called to live in connectedness with other believers as well as with God. We are individual members of the body of Christ, living and functioning in a network of healthy, interdependent relationships with the other members. We need one another, and although we all partake of the same Spirit, we must learn to appreciate the diversity of gifting and function that each believer provides to the Church as a unified body. It is important to remember that believers of every nation have equal access to the throne of God and enjoy the privilege of praying along with every other child of God—"Our Father."

1. Write down any qualities about your earthly father and mother that have truly blessed your life. Multiply them by 10,000 and then apply them to your image of your Father in heaven. If you can, tell your folks about your list.

2. Think about the ways in which your earthly father and mother have come up short, both as people and as parents. Do this not to become embittered, but to consider prayerfully how you may have unfairly transferred these shortcomings onto your image of God. Ask Him to forgive you for doing this and to show you how He is different than you have imagined.

3. Ask the most godly and spiritually mature man or woman you know to pray with you to be able to better comprehend what your heavenly Father is really like.

4. Call God "Papa" or "Daddy" sometimes when you pray. Keep doing it until it feels right and normal.

Great God in the heavens, please reveal to me Your Fatherhood over my life. I confess You as the source of all good things, both visible and invisible. I know that my true life is in You alone. Thank You for choosing me, setting Your love upon me long before I ever loved You and adopting me as Your own. Remind me that my meaning and significance come from my identity as Your child— that "whose I am" informs me of "who I am." You are my security, and You hold my true identity in Your hands. I praise You, for You have neither left me alone nor left me to myself. You have given me the gift of life.

You have planted the seed of Your living word within me. You have called me to be a vessel that is useful to You. Help me to trust more deeply in Your oversight of my life. I release a wrong control over my life to You. At the same time, I want to embrace a proper responsibility for it. I desire to be childlike in spirit and yet put away childish things. I want to learn what pleases You—not simply what will keep me from grieving You. Father, I long to bring a smile to Your face when You consider my life and my ways. I love You already and want to love You even more.

Help me to cooperate with Your plan for my transformation into the image of Jesus. Father, I want to embrace the necessary trials and pains You ordain that will keep me trusting in You from the depths of my heart. I submit myself to Your great wisdom and loving leadership over my life. Empower me to obey You as a loving child does a generous daddy. Please deal gently with me, and help me to listen and respond quickly when Your Spirit convicts me of sin, righteousness and judgment. Father, please let me see Your smile. In the precious name of Jesus I pray. Amen.

Prayer for laborers in the harvest

But when He saw the multitudes, He was moved with compassion for them, because they were weary and scattered, like sheep having no shepherd. Then He said to His disciples, "The harvest truly is plentiful, but the laborers are few. Therefore pray the Lord of the harvest to send out laborers into His harvest."

—MATTHEW 9:36–38

Prayer for the Holy Spirit's ministry

If you then, being evil, know how to give good gifts to your children, how much more will your heavenly Father give the Holy Spirit to those who ask Him!

—LUKE 11:13

Prayer for justice and right to prevail

Then He spoke a parable to them, that men always ought to pray and not lose heart, saying: "There was in a certain city a judge who did not fear God nor regard man. Now there was a widow in that city; and she came to him, saying, 'Get justice for me from my adversary.' And he would not for a while; but afterward he said within himself, 'Though I do not fear God nor regard man, yet because this widow troubles me I will avenge her, lest by her continual coming she weary me.'"

Then the Lord said, "Hear what the unjust judge said. And shall God not avenge His own elect who cry out day and night to Him, though He bears long with them? I tell you that He will avenge them speedily. Nevertheless, when the Son of Man comes, will He really find faith on the earth?"

—LUKE 18:1–8

A Parable Regarding the Power of Many Prayers

I once heard this true story recounted.

> Years ago an English ship sank in the harbor of a city in southern Asia. There was a very valuable, very large bell the ship had been transporting that had gone down with the ship. Try as they might by many means and attempts, the crew members were unsuccessful in recovering it. They gave it up as a loss.
>
> A native man in the city asked if the town could have the bell as its own if he could raise it off of the floor of the bay. The English ship captain agreed to this with a degree of amusement. He knew that these people didn't have any machines available to help them accomplish this impossible feat.
>
> The man then conscripted seven dozen divers to take turns diving down to the bell. He had each swimmer carry with him a hollow lightweight reed and then place it underneath the bell. After hundreds and hundreds of dives a particular diver placed one more reed under the giant bell, and lo and behold, the bell came rising to the surface of the waters.

We will have petitions before God for which we plead before His throne of mercy. It is right and good that we agree in prayer for specific needs with other members of the body of Christ. The prayers of many will be more powerful than the prayers of few. And, we never know; maybe our prayer will serve to be the very one that evokes the divine response that has been accruing since the hour that the first believer's request for that particular need to be met came before God.

> And the smoke of the incense, with the prayers of the saints, ascended before God from the angel's hand. Then the angel took the censer, filled it with fire from the altar, and threw it to the earth. And there were noises, thunderings, lightnings, and an earthquake.
>
> —REVELATION 8:4–5

Two

"Which Art in Heaven"

Prayer Element—Worship

We Sing

One word from Your mouth
And the heavens were made
You breathed and the stars filled the sky
God strong and mighty The Ancient of Days
On the wings of the wind You ride
We sing and we dance

You cause the barren desert to bloom
Turn the sea into dry land
Your voice has raised the dead from the tomb
Evil flees when You command

CHORUS
We sing we dance we clap and cry out
We kneel we bow we shout
We declare the Kingdom of our God

All of creation exalts in Your name
Trees of the field clap their hands
The earth shouts for joy even mountains sing
The redeemed of the Lord lift their hands

And sing we dance we clap cry out
We kneel we bow we shout we praise (repeat)
We declare the Kingdom of our God

Draw Me Closer

My spirit is yearning to be with You
To rest in Your presence to be renewed
My heart is searching for Your chambers
To worship You
One holy passion for communion Lord

CHORUS
Draw me closer to Your heart
Draw me close to You (repeat)
Draw me closer to Your heart
Draw me close to You (repeat)

You fashioned within me this thirst for You
To drink of the water which flows from You
And I hunger for the bread of Heaven
Your breath of life
I seek Your holy habitation Lord

(Repeat chorus)

My Savior I love You I worship You
Redeemer how I long to be with You

(Repeat chorus)

The simple phrase, "Our Father *in heaven*," that our Lord Jesus Christ taught us to pray relates in part to the nature and location of God's presence in this universe. As we consider this theme, we are indeed touching a great and marvelous mystery. What mortal human can fully grasp the truths that surround such a weighty subject? Even so, great insight is available to us from the teaching of Scripture regarding the dwelling place of God.

Many Bible teachers have noted well the marvelous comparison between our having both a *good Father*, who is close at hand (the immanence of God), and a *great King*, who rules over all things from heaven (the transcendence of God). This is certainly a helpful way of thinking of "Our Father in heaven" and what it implies. However, heaven is not only "up there somewhere" and "far away." Heaven can also be understood as nearby—a dimension "right next door" to this realm we can perceive by our senses. "Heaven" can actually break through and manifest itself in our earthly realm at any time God pleases. It is from this angle of the nearness of God's heavenly presence to us that I will write this chapter, for I believe that for too many people, a consciousness of heaven is too far removed from their life on earth.

GOD'S OMNIPRESENCE

In wonder, King David asks God:

> Where can I go from Your Spirit? Or where can I flee from Your presence? If I ascend into heaven, You are there; if I make my bed in hell, behold, You are there. If I take the wings of the morning, and dwell in the uttermost parts of the sea, even there Your hand shall lead me, and Your right hand shall hold me.
>
> —PSALM 139:7–10

Your Kingdom Come

At the time King Solomon dedicated the temple that he had built for God, he inquired with inspiration:

> But will God indeed dwell on the earth? Behold, heaven and the heaven of heavens cannot contain You. How much less this temple which I have built! Yet regard the prayer of Your servant and his supplication, O LORD my God, and listen to the cry and the prayer which Your servant is praying before You today.
>
> —1 KINGS 8:27–28

There are many possible Bible passages that would communicate the same reality—God is everywhere at the same time. God is *omnipresent*. He is the unavoidable God!

We can draw a helpful word picture from our knowledge of the physical atmosphere to help us conceive the truths of God's omnipresence. Where can we go to avoid air or space? Air and space are all around us. Beyond our atmosphere, outer space continues on infinitely. God's presence is as near to us as the air we breathe. God's presence is simultaneously near the most distant galaxy in the universe. Since God is everywhere, God is also nearby all things. Most often when people think of God being "in heaven," they think of Him only as being "far, far away" from us and the affairs of our planet. This is most unfortunate and "far, far away" from the truth. The literal word that Jesus uses for heaven in the Lord's Prayer is actually in the plural form—"Our Father in the *heavens*." Maybe this speaks of the various dimensions and forms in which "heaven" exists.

PRAYERFACT 3

—Prayerfact 2 (see page 29)

Our earthly existence is a gift from God that confers upon us a true freedom as real persons in God's great universe.

—Prayerfact 4 (see page 49)

In his excellent book titled *New Testament Theology,* Donald Guthrie makes these following observations, among many others, about the meanings and use of the word *heaven* in the New Testament:[1]

- The many references to heaven as the abode of God are an important factor in the New Testament.

- The root idea is *habitation* in all the words used of heaven in both the Old and New Testaments.

- Localized expressions (such as "above," "up" or "ascend") must be recognized to be due to the limitations of human language to express the supramundane.

- Heaven was for Jesus synonymous with His Father's presence; it possessed no sense of remoteness.

- God is other than earthbound, i.e., not restricted to the limitations of material creation. This explains also the voice from heaven (Matt. 3:17; Mark 1:11; Luke 3:21–22) and the activity of Jesus in looking up to heaven when in prayer.

- Jesus never enlarged on the idea of location; it is not important. Heaven is where God is.

- Heaven is clearly linked to the will of God.

- In the Book of Acts, the few times heaven is mentioned almost invariably either denotes the firmament above the earth, or it is practically a substitute expression for God.

- Peter and Paul both heard voices from heaven.

- Stephen saw the heavens opened (Acts 7:55).

- Jesus ascended into heaven and will return out of heaven (Acts 1:9–11; 3:21).

- Heaven is the dwelling place of God (Acts 7:48–49).

- Paul speaks of being caught up to the third heaven where he was given revelations of the Lord (2 Cor. 12).

- The Book of Hebrews links the idea of a city to the conception of heaven (Heb. 11:10, 16; 12:22).

- Heaven is conceived as a city, even though built by humans, because cities are highly expressive of the concept of community. Cities cannot exist on isolationism; they depend on cooperation.

- Heaven is the home of the Holy Spirit and the risen Christ, who is at the right hand of God with angels, authorities and powers subject to Him (1 Pet. 1:12; 3:22).

- Heaven is closely linked to the glory of God.

To me, the main point seems to be that God's presence permeates our whole universe, from the heavens just *about us* to the heavens *light-years away*. Because God is everywhere, heaven is always potentially very nearby, for heaven is where God is.

God's Manifest Presence

All around us there is a spiritual world, normally invisible to us, that interfaces with the physical world much more than most of us realize. From time to time, people do get glimpses into this spirit world. Some people do this by practicing the occult. This is soundly forbidden by the teaching of all of Holy Scripture. (See Deuteronomy 18:10–12; 2 Chronicles 33:6.) Periodically though, the Holy Spirit's operation will initiate and grant God's people such glimpses into the spirit world.

At times, God is pleased to manifest His presence in the physical realm. He is in the business of performing *miracles* (unusual acts of His power) as well as exercising *providence* (usual acts of His power). Miracles are demonstrations of the power of heaven breaking into the earthly realm. Besides other important reasons, God periodically, and more often than we tend to imagine, performs miracles as *reminders* to us that He exercises His providential power all around us day and night. He "[upholds] all things by the word of His power" (Heb. 1:3).

Although God is omnipresent, this does not hinder Him from localizing His presence in the form of His choice. The Holy Spirit descended and rested upon Jesus in the form of a dove at His baptism. And of course, the Incarnation of God the Son, Jesus Christ, is the most vivid example of this phenomenon. The eternal and invisible word of God "became flesh and dwelt among us" (John 1:14).

The exact line between the interrelationship of matter and spirit has not yet been fully discerned by humankind. In this fallen age, we find it difficult to find the proper continuity between spirit and matter. C. S. Lewis expressed this struggle well:

> When nature and spirit are fully harmonized—when spirit rides nature so perfectly that the two together make rather a Centaur than a mounted knight...there will be no room to get the finest razor blade of thought in between spirit and nature. Every state of affairs in the new nature will be the perfect expression of the spiritual state and every spiritual state the perfect informing of, and bloom upon, a state of affairs; one with it as the perfume with a flower or the spirit of great poetry with its form.[2]

It is interesting to note that the word *supernatural,* used by so many Christians today to describe miracles, is never used in the Bible. It's not that it's a bad word, but it does speak to a general loss of our awareness that everything that exists is continually sustained by the power of God. It also betrays a hidden belief among us that miracles are somehow "unnatural." To the early Christians, miracles were "supernaturally natural"—a more regular and expected part of Christian living and normal church life. We need to return to the faith of our fathers! This understanding of God's presence among us is also vitally connected to a life of prayer. Why would we pray fervently to a God who is unwilling or who finds it difficult or impossible to break into the affairs of humanity?

I deeply believe that a joint celebration on the part of Christians of the omnipresence of God and the manifest presence of God is called for in Scripture. The first believers lived with the consciousness of both realities and expected that the God who is truly omnipresent will also oftentimes manifest His presence and perform "signs and wonders." *Signs* point to things beyond themselves—in this case to the living God whose glory among people is the reason for their performance. *Wonders* cause people to stop in the tracks of their unbelief and wonder at what the great God behind them must really be like.

God's personality is truly marvelous to consider. Every sin can ultimately be traced to some misconception of God. The true and intimate knowledge of God has the power to greatly change human life for the good. It stands to reason that Jesus would say in John 17:3, "This is eternal life, that they may know You, the only true God, and Jesus Christ whom You have sent." The true knowledge of God is actually the very essence of eternal life.

TRANSCENDENCE, IMMANENCE AND THE GENIUS OF GOD

When the apostle Paul was preaching to the philosophers in Athens, he declared, "God, who made the world and everything in it, since He is Lord of heaven and earth, does not dwell in temples made with hands. Nor is He worshiped with men's hands, as though He needed anything, since He gives to all life, breath, and all things" (Acts 17:24–25). A moment later he adds, "For in Him we live and move and have our being" (v. 28). Theologians have referred to God as being both transcendent and immanent. That is, He is above and beyond all things, while at the same time, He is intimately involved with the earth and its inhabitants—He is "the Lord of heaven and earth." There are two very popular world-views that exist today and have been around a long time. One is called *deism,* and the other is called *monism.* Deists believe God is far removed from His creation—that He has much more important matters to attend to in His vast "multi-verse." They can relate to the concept of the transcendence of God, but not to His immanence. Monists believe that everything is a part of God. They can relate to the concept of His immanence, but not His transcendence (i.e., How dare anyone suggest that God is above and beyond creation?). The Bible presents God as possessing both attributes simultaneously. Wow! Only the true God could come up with such a dynamic duo! Only such a God is worthy of our worship.

When Isaiah saw the Lord high and lifted up with the train of His robe filling the temple, he was allowed to witness the seraph cry out to another like it, "Holy, holy, holy is the LORD of hosts." The word *holy* speaks of the transcendent majesty of God. Yet, in the very next line, the marvelous creature stated, "The whole earth is full of His glory!" (Isa. 6:1–3). This speaks of God's glorious presence and actions that permeate our world. Doesn't it seem somewhat strange that the seraph who is caught up in the blazing glory of that awesome heavenly realm would mention our little planet in the same breath by which it declares the holiness of our Creator? Nevertheless, it did! Maybe the drama of our earthly existence is more important in heaven's eyes than we would naturally tend to think.

GOD WANTS US

Not only is God *omnipresent* (everywhere present), He is *omniscient* (all-knowing) as well. And not only is God omniscient, He is *omnipotent* (all-powerful) as well. The apostle Paul said, "[There is] one God and Father of all, who is above all, and through all, and in you all" (Eph. 4:6). Yet standing out among these awesome attributes that tend to overwhelm us, the apostle John simply says, "God is love" (1 John 4:16). Now this is something about God that draws us close to His great heart. God is totally self-sufficient, yet He also possesses passionate desires within His heart. Although He doesn't *need* anything, He *wants* many things. He especially wants fellowship with human beings just like us. However, He does not coerce our love or affection; He wants to be freely wanted and loved by us. If you have ever wanted to be wanted by someone, you have experienced a sliver of the agony and ecstasy intertwined in the heart of God regarding humankind.

All of God's acts as the Master of creation, human history and geopolitics have been for the purpose that people would gain this wisdom to seek after and connect with Him. "And He has made from one blood every nation of men to dwell on all the face of the earth, and has determined their preappointed times and the boundaries of their dwellings, so that they should seek the Lord, in the hope that they might grope for Him and find Him, though He is not far from each one of us; for in Him we live and move and have our being" (Acts 17:26–28). True love is voluntary by nature. God's hope is that every person in every nation of every generation might choose to seek after Him and fall in love with Him through receiving and following His Son Jesus Christ. God not only hopes for the finding, but He has even ordained the groping after Him ("the hope to grope"). The *journey* is as essential as the *destination* for our full development as humans. We should validate people's search for God, for if it is present, it is a sign that God is already working by His grace in their souls. We know this because no person left alone without divine influence seeks after God (Rom. 3:11).

LIVING IN TWO REALMS

Another important truth about our Father's dwelling place in the heavens is that it is the realm in which His highest will and glory are fully expressed. Later in the Lord's Prayer Jesus refers to this very thing, "Your will be done on earth as it is in heaven" (Matt. 6:10). *Heaven* is ultimately the realm of absolute perfection and well-being. It is from this spiritual and invisible realm that the material and visible world was actually made. "By faith we

48

understand that the worlds were framed by the word of God, so that the things which are seen were not made of things which are visible" (Heb. 11:3). The philosophical implication of this is not that the visible realm is bad and only the invisible realm is good. Rather, it is that the invisible is to be *dominant* over the visible and the visible *subordinate* to the invisible. This is the divine order for life.

In order to live out our lives well here upon the earth, the apostle Paul informs us that we are not to "look at the things which are seen, but at the things which are not seen. For the things which are seen are temporary, but the things which are not seen are eternal" (2 Cor. 4:18). The eternal realities of the invisible realm are to become the actual hidden source of power and wisdom for living our human lives well within this material world. This is why the apostle Paul prayed for believers to have "the eyes of [their] understanding" enlightened to the nature of the hope of God's calling upon them (Eph. 1:18). Christians are already "seated . . . with Him in the heavenly places" (Eph. 2:6, NAS) even though we still "walk in the flesh" (2 Cor. 10:3)—that is, we are still living in this fallen age. We live in the present realities of two realms—heaven and earth—and in two ages—this one and the one to come.

This principle of having faith in the invisible God and His invisible, yet readily accessible, kingdom was the primary key to the successful lives of the heroes of faith who are honored in Hebrews 11. Like Moses, they all prevailed and endured by "seeing Him who is invisible," and therefore God was "not ashamed to be called their God" (Heb. 11:27, 16). We are

---

PRAYERFACT 4

—Prayerfact 3 (see page 42)

God is limited only by the loving choice He has made to allow other volitional beings to truly exist and live real lives in His universe.

—Prayerfact 5 (see page 60)

---

called to the same way of life in Christ. As Christians, we are alert and alive to the powers of heaven that are not far from any one of us and also to the realities of the God-loved and blessed, but fallen, world around us and to the complications this tension poses for both our lives and the lives of people scattered across the nations of the earth.

When we pray to our heavenly Father, we are praying to the One who, although invisible, is not far from any of us. He is the One who sees all things clearly and knows all things perfectly. He is the One who dwells in a realm of absolute love and power. He is the One who passionately longs to interact with us even more than we desire to interact with Him. And He is the One who has the rightful claim to reign as King over us all, for He has given us life, breath and all good things, and not we ourselves. We are His flock and the sheep of His pasture — our great and good Father in the heavens.

1. Go outside away from the city lights on a clear night and look at the stars. Think about the intelligence and power it took for God to create each star and then link them together in a panoramic display of His glory. Contemplate infinity, and then contemplate God's infinite nature.

2. Think about the reality that because you now exist, you will never cease to exist.

3. Imagine living forever with totally perfect people as a perfect person in the immediate presence of God in a perfect environment. Think about anything and everything in this life that tends to "get you down," and then think of heaven as a place where none of these experiences can possibly be had. Then call to mind all the pleasurable experiences you can experience in this life and try to conceive that these things cannot begin to compare to the pleasures in the age to come.

A Prayer from the Heart

O God, who is like You? You are above and beyond all creation, and yet You bend low to care so compassionately for all You have made. Give me eyes to perceive Your omnipresence and the ability of heart to trust that You are always nearby—that at all times, I truly live and move and have my very being in You. Never allow me to forget that there is absolutely nowhere that I can go to escape Your presence. Indeed, may I never want to escape it.

Lord, You are just a humble whisper away even when You seem to hide Your face. I ask that You will, time and again, manifest Your presence in and around my life and ministry to others. Show Your glory and power, and cause the hearts of many to marvel at You and Your work in the earth. Make me a person of Your presence who is, at once, not uncomfortable in it, nor overly familiar with it. You are the King—eternal, immortal, invisible—the only wise God who dwells in unapproachable light. To You be all glory, honor, dominion, riches, blessing, praise and power forever. Amen.

Jesus' high priestly prayer

Father, the hour has come. Glorify Your Son, that Your Son also may glorify You, as You have given Him authority over all flesh, that He should give eternal life to as many as You have given Him. And this is eternal life, that they may know You, the only true God, and Jesus Christ whom You have sent. I have glorified You on the earth. I have finished the work which You have given Me to do. And now, O Father, glorify Me together with Yourself, with the glory which I had with You before the world was.

I have manifested Your name to the men whom You have given Me out of the world. They were Yours, You gave them to Me, and they have kept Your word. Now they have known that all things which You have given Me are from You. For I have given to them the words which You have given Me; and they have received them, and have known surely that I came forth from You; and they have believed that You sent Me.

I pray for them. I do not pray for the world but for those whom You have given Me, for they are Yours. And all Mine are Yours, and Yours are Mine, and I am glorified in them. Now I am no longer in the world, but these are in the world, and I come to You. Holy Father, keep through Your name those whom You have given Me, that they may be one as We are. While I was with them in the world, I kept them in Your name. Those whom You gave Me I have kept; and none of them is lost except the son of perdition, that the Scripture might be fulfilled. But now I come to You, and these things I speak in the world, that they may have My joy fulfilled in themselves. I have given them Your word; and the world has hated them because they are not of the world, just as I am not of the world. I do not pray that You should take them out of the world, but that You should keep them from the evil one. They are not of the world, just as I am not of the world.

Sanctify them by Your truth. Your word is truth. As You sent Me into the world, I also have sent them into the world. And for their sakes I sanctify Myself, that they also may be sanctified by the truth.

I do not pray for these alone, but also for those who will believe in Me through their word; that they all may be one, as You, Father, are in Me, and I in You; that they also may be one in Us, that the world may believe that You sent Me. And the glory which You gave Me I have given them, that they may be one just as We are one: I in them, and You in Me; that they may be made perfect in one, and that the world may know that You have sent Me, and have loved them as You have loved Me.

Father, I desire that they also whom You gave Me may be with Me where I am, that they may behold My glory which You have given Mc; for You loved Me before the foundation of the world. O righteous Father! The world has not known You, but I have known You; and these have known that You sent Me. And I have declared to them Your name, and will declare it, that the love with which You loved Me may be in them, and I in them.

—JOHN 17:1–26

Three

"Hallowed Be Thy Name"

Prayer Element—Worship

Adonai

Almighty Most Holy our Lord our God
We bow down we worship our Lord our God
Adonai Elohim God Most High

Hallowed, sacred, revered, venerated, holy, exalted and treasured above all else—these concepts have fallen on hard times in our secularized culture. There are, however, some indications that many people in our society are getting in touch with the blight and barrenness of soul that secularism has left in its wake. There is a growing hunger in the Western world, although often misguided, to reestablish a spiritual connection with God in our earthly existence. A brief glance around today's bookstores quickly confirms this point. This is an opportune hour for Christians to manifest to the Christ-ignoring world the superior love, transforming power and way of life associated with the gospel of our Lord Jesus. Such an awakening of genuine spirituality is the only hope for our devolving, neopagan and postmodern culture.

The hallowedness, or holiness, of God's name implies His eternal separateness and otherness in relation to all other things. All else that exists in this universe has been created by the Trinitarian God of the Bible who Himself is uncreated. This fact forever sets Him apart and qualifies Him alone as the proper object of worship by all of creation. Our human hearts have been divinely designed for worship—the history of world religions is the best confirmation of this. How marvelous it is that there truly is Someone—not just a "something"—absolutely holy for us to worship. Someone who made us, loves us, has sacrificed Himself for us and who has the will and power to hear and answer our prayers.

In our strenuous effort to make all things equally valuable and legitimate as required by the humanistic and powerful guilt-manipulators of our era, we have, as a whole, gradually forfeited the profound personal and societal influence that flows from being conscious of the divine. To falsely imagine all things equal is to devalue what is best. Rather than everything being lifted up, as the engineers of egalitarianism would vainly hope, everything actually becomes debased. By imagining that all things are equally valid and good, these "powers that be" are in serious denial of the very real presence of evil in this world. There are some things that are intrinsically superior to other things. Christians are exhorted in Scripture to "approve the things that are excellent" and to meditate upon the things that are true, noble, just, pure, lovely, of good report, virtuous or praiseworthy (Phil. 1:10; 4:8). There are other things in this world that can be contemplated!

God is calling the body of Christ to extract once again the precious from the vile and to discern between the holy and the profane (Jer. 15:19). The natural order only takes its proper place in human experience

> **PRAYERFACT 5**
>
> —Prayerfact 4 (see page 49)
>
> *The dignity of all human life is derived from the gift of freedom bestowed upon us by God. It is a reflection that we, in a unique way, bear the image and likeness of God Himself.*
>
> —Prayerfact 6 (see page 64)

when it is clothed from on high and meshed with life in the Spirit of God. Otherwise, what is natural becomes dominant as it flows in to fill the vacuum created by the rejection of the Spirit's dominion. By this dynamic, natural human life tends to become progressively perverted in its expressions. Created things automatically become *false religious idols* in this scenario, for we can never successfully deny our instinctive longing and impulse to worship—even if we limit ourselves to worshiping creations of our own design or imagination.

HUMILITY AND WORSHIP

It is in order to rectify and realign the human heart's tendency to exalt vanity that the Master of Life teaches us to pray, *"Hallowed be Your name."* Our lives will not take on authentic meaning unless we regard as sacred the name of God and set Him above all other things in our affections. By understanding this reality, we are properly humbled. And it is to the humble that God gives grace. *Humility does not mean stooping to pretend that we are less than we actually are. Rather, it is standing alongside the One who is infinitely more than we are without denying the reality of the contrast.*

In reference to the resurrected Christ, the writer of Hebrews declares, " . . . who is holy, harmless, undefiled, separate from sinners, and has become higher than the heavens . . . " (Heb. 7:26). If this is true of the Son, it is certainly also true of the Father. We can never be satisfied in the depths of our souls unless there is such a God in this universe to exalt and adore. All other aspects of human existence become rightly informed and naturally fall into their proper place if this first priority is embraced from the heart.

WHAT'S IN A NAME?

In biblical culture, names meant much more than they do in our modern culture. A name was often symbolically invested with the very nature, character and personality of the person bearing the label. In fact, Jesus could summarize His whole earthly mission in the statement, "And I have declared to them Your name, and will declare it, that the love with which You loved Me may be in them, and I in them" (John 17:26). That is why Solomon said that to revere and esteem the name of God is the beginning of wisdom (Prov. 9:10). The name of the Father revealed to us has the power to impart to our souls the same quality of love for Jesus that the Father Himself has for Jesus.

This intimate knowledge of God's name obviously means more than being able to pronounce the name *YHWH!* We need to know Him on an experiential level. To "know" another in scriptural language was used as a code word for having sexual relations with that person. Of course I am not intimating that we ever will have sex with God (the very thought seems blasphemous), but we are called the bride of Christ and our relationship to the holy Trinity is certainly spiritually romantic in nature. The apostle Paul stated that the relationship between Christ and His church is mirrored on earth by the relationship

Your Kingdom Come

between a husband and a wife. He then referred to this as a great mystery. (See Ephesians 5:23–32.)

To *hallow* the name of God is to know deeply and celebrate His personality, identity, character, reputation, fame, wealth and nature. Moreover, it implies that we are to be moved to the very depths of our personalities by our awareness of God's name. Our wills, minds and emotions are all radically affected by such knowledge, as are how we daily manage our bodies, our time, our talents, our treasures and our interpersonal relationships.

GOD'S "PROPER" NAME

What actually is God's "proper" name? Strictly speaking, there is only one proper name of God revealed to us in Scripture. Words like *El* were used, which could refer not only to the one true God, but also to false "gods." *El* was used very much as we use the word *god* in English. The personal name used in Scripture for God is *YHWH*. In most English translations of the Bible it is rendered as LORD. Calling *YHWH* "my Lord" (*Adonai* in Hebrew) became a practice in late Old Testament times because God's proper name was viewed as so sacred that the Jews of that time would not say it aloud. Ironically, because of this piece of history, we have lost the official pronunciation of *YHWH*. Even today, many religious Jews write *G-d* instead of spelling out G-o-d. Some English translations of the Bible translate *YHWH* as *Jehovah*. This practice, which combines the consonants of *YHWH* and the vowels of *Adonai*, began in medieval Europe.

Much more important than the pronunciation or translation of God's name is the simple yet profound meaning of *YHWH*. It is derived from the verb "to be." *YHWH* was the name by which God revealed Himself to Moses at the burning bush:

> And God said to Moses, "I AM WHO I AM." And He said, "Thus you shall say to the children of Israel, 'I AM has sent me to you.'"
>
> —EXODUS 3:14

62

The living God had previously revealed this personal name to the patriarchs, but He gave Moses a *deeper insight into and a demonstration of* the power of His name as God delivered the children of Israel out of Egypt by unprecedented signs and wonders:

> Then the LORD said to Moses, "Now you shall see what I will do to Pharaoh. For with a strong hand he will let them go, and with a strong hand he will drive them out of his land." And God spoke to Moses and said to him: "I am the LORD. I appeared to Abraham, to Isaac, and to Jacob, as God Almighty, but by My name LORD I was not known to them."
>
> —EXODUS 6:1–3

The fact that God has chosen His name to be "I Am" has tremendous implications for our life of prayer. He is not the great "I Used to Be," "I Used to Do," "I Will One Day Be" or "I Will Someday Do." He is alive and is "the same yesterday, today, and forever" (Heb. 13:8). The infinite and eternal One has condescended to relate genuinely to us in the present tense and has committed Himself to hear and answer our prayers offered through the Spirit's power in the name of His Son, Jesus Christ. *God is* right now, and He is near to us—He has always been and He will always be.

THE "HYPHENATED NAMES" OF GOD

In the Old Testament, there were times when descriptive titles were added to God's name Jehovah. These were not new names of God; they simply provided further insight into *YHWH*'s personality and nature. These names were revealed in the context of the historical events that accompanied the manifestation of a particular personality trait or attribute that *YHWH* possesses. *Jehovah-jireh* (the LORD our provider), *Jehovah-shalom* (the LORD our peace), *Jehovah-tsidkenu* (the LORD our righteousness), *Jehovah-rophe* (the LORD our healer), *Jehovah-shammah* (the LORD is there), the LORD of Hosts, the LORD God of Israel

> ### PRAYERFACT 6
>
> —Prayerfact 5 (see page 60)
>
> *In addition to our natural life, God's plan is for us to enjoy partaking of His life—a higher and eternal kind of life that connects and meshes our limited human powers to and with the limitless powers of the kingdom of heaven.*
>
> —Prayerfact 7 (see page 84)

and the Holy One of Israel are among these divine titles.

In choosing to call Himself "I Am," God is declaring to all humanity that He reserves the right to define Himself to us, and therefore we do not have the right to define Him for ourselves. *God is*—He just is, and we all know it down deep in our hearts. And He will be who He will be. He has always been, and He will forever be—without beginning or end. Maybe the deeper question we need to answer is, *Who does He say we are in His universe?* God doesn't have to justify His existence to us, and He never attempts to, although He has graciously left us many evidences, both internal and external, of His real presence among us and beyond us.

SPREADING THE FAME OF HIS NAME

To pray for God's name to be hallowed has another very important application that must not be overlooked. By this prayer, we are also asking God to empower us to spread His fame and the fame of His Son to the ends of the earth. We are His ambassadors who bear the good news of who He is and what He has done by His great power and might throughout the ages. It is not just we who are called to hallow His name— every creature is called to worship the living God. Before human history is complete, God will be loved and adored by people from every nation, tribe, tongue and family on the planet.

The whole earth needs to hear of the greatness of God and the beauty of Jesus Christ. Creation is waiting on its tiptoes to hear the story of the Bridegroom/King who left the riches of

His heavenly home to rescue His chosen bride from the clutches of an ancient and evil dragon by sacrificing His life and then rising to life again. Many will open their hearts to believe that they are a part of that chosen and colorful bride, who is comprised of multitudes of people from every tribe on the face of the earth.

God has called those who have so believed to be His appointed messengers to those who have not yet heard of the love that this Bridegroom/King has for them. This is the divine privilege bestowed upon believers. He has sent us forth with His power and authority as living witnesses of His message to humanity. We are even allowed to suffer reproach for His name at the hands of those who resist His love. Whatever else we are called by God to do in this life, this undergirding ambassadorial calling is to be our primary vocation. We can fulfill this divine mandate by living, speaking and shining for Him while we go about our normal lives wherever and in whatever circumstances God has placed us by His providential wisdom. Don't wait to share His message of beautiful love—begin today with the people all about you. *God has sent you to them!*

1. Ask God to show you the ways He will help you, both now and in the coming days, to spread His fame throughout the earth. Commit yourself to cooperate with His plan.

2. When you find it hard to focus while praying, think of God as being right in the room with you, listening to every word you are saying. Put your effort into saying what is truly on your mind and heart.

3. Ask God to work alongside of you for an entire day in every situation. Watch for His activities, and record in a journal anything that you believe that God might have accomplished.

Father, Son and Holy Spirit, I confess that "You are"—You have always been and You always will be—the one true God in trinity. Who could ever negate You? It is because of You that all other things and all other beings exist. I praise You that You have no need to prove that You are. Thank You for providing such powerful witnesses for us—both internal and external—regarding Your presence in this universe. I set You apart in my heart as the Lord of the heavens and the earth. You are my Lord.

Your name is far above all other "powers that be"—the heavenly host, the powers of darkness, the powers of creation, the kings of the earth and the might of all humanity. All these will one day confess Your dominion and bow before You. You have betrothed me to You, and I gladly and willingly lay my name aside to take yours upon me. What an honor You have bestowed upon me and all who call upon Your name with a brave and genuine heart. Let me be known by Your name. I will not be ashamed to confess You before all creation. Your Good News is the very power of God for the salvation all people. Demonstrate the glory and power of Your name in this evil age. Make the name of Jesus Christ the Son famous in all the earth—and let the nations be glad. Amen.

Prayer for signs and wonders to confirm the gospel

"Now, Lord, look on their threats, and grant to Your servants that with all boldness they may speak Your word, by stretching out Your hand to heal, and that signs and wonders may be done through the name of Your holy Servant Jesus." And when they had prayed, the place where they were assembled together was shaken; and they were all filled with the Holy Spirit, and they spoke the word of God with boldness.

—ACTS 4:29–31

Prayer for impartation of spiritual gifts

For God is my witness, whom I serve with my spirit in the gospel of His Son, that without ceasing I make mention of you always in my prayers, making request if, by some means, now at last I may find a way in the will of God to come to you. For I long to see you, that I may impart to you some spiritual gift, so that you may be established—that is, that I may be encouraged together with you by the mutual faith both of you and me.

—ROMANS 1:9–12

Prayer for the lost to be converted

Brethren, my heart's desire and prayer to God for Israel is that they may be saved.

—ROMANS 10:1

Prayer for unity in the Church

Now may the God of patience and comfort grant you to be like-minded toward one another, according to Christ Jesus, that you may with one mind and one mouth glorify the God and Father of our Lord Jesus Christ.

—ROMANS 15:5–6

Prayer for spiritual hope for believers

Now may the God of hope fill you with all joy and peace in believing, that you may abound in hope by the power of the Holy Spirit.

—ROMANS 15:13

Prayer for peace and God's nearness

Now the God of peace be with you all. Amen.

—ROMANS 15:33

Praying for Israel According to the Pattern Prayer[1]

Jesus taught His disciples to pray, "Our Father…hallowed be Your name" (Luke 11:2). These words are not a cue for preparatory praise prior to entering God's presence. They are an impassioned plea for the "sanctifying of God's name" that will occur when His reign is realized. This is the pivotal and foundational petition of prayer. Everything else in the prayer is dependent upon and an extension of this petition.

To pray this prayer as originally intended we must identify with the disciples. What was the life situation of Yeshua and His disciples when this prayer was given?

The Jewish people in the land of Israel were dominated, humiliated and cruelly oppressed by Rome. They were divided into various sects vying for religious dominance. In addition, they were scattered and oppressed among the nations. Objects of scorn and discrimination at home and abroad, Israel groaned beneath this heathen yoke. The faithful Israelite was threatened by priestly apostasy and surrounded by heathen darkness.

The Jews believed that God would restore Israel in the Messianic kingdom. In that kingdom God's will would be entirely expressed and His name would be absolutely "hallowed."

With this in mind, let us consider what the "hallowing" of God's name meant to Messiah and the Jewish apostles.

GOD'S NAME

In the Book of Psalms we find that individuals asked God, "for His name's sake," to forgive (25:11), to lead and guide (31:3), to help and deliver (79:9) and to instruct and unite the petitioner's heart (86:11–12).

Jesus and His disciples had their understandings formed and framed by the Word of God. It was prophesied of the Messiah that He would "meditate" upon the Scriptures "day and night." With that in mind, let's explore various Scriptures.

The concept of God's name in Scripture was well developed

theologically. Initially God's name was identified with God's presence. His name communicated God's nature and activity. It was something "tangible" in which a person could place his faith, for "whoever calls on the name of the LORD shall be saved" (Joel 2:32).

At Sinai God forbade the construction and worship of images. The tabernacle "imaged" God's presence with His people. It was where God's name dwelled.

Its successor was Solomon's Temple. This was looked forward to in Deuteronomy 12:11 and was seen as the fulfillment of God's determination to have a house for His name (1 Kings 3:2; 5:3).

Eventually, God's name became a synonym for His person. (See Psalm 20:1, 5, 7; 44:5; Isaiah 30:27.)

GOD'S NAME AND ISRAEL

God's reputation was inextricably bound to His people's condition. Therefore, prayer for Israel's restoration was ultimately for the glory of God's name. His name being honored is connected in 2 Samuel 7:25–26 to the fulfillment of God's promise—the Davidic (Messianic) kingdom.

The prophets saw the glory of God's name as being tied up with Israel's condition. For the sake of God's name Jeremiah desperately pleaded with God to do something for Judah (Jer. 14:7). He pleaded with God not to abhor (despise) them (Jer. 14:21). Daniel prayed for Israel's restoration for the sake of God's name (Dan. 9:18–19).

In Psalm 115 we read anguished intercession that for the glory of His name the nations mocking Israel would be silenced. In Scripture we constantly see the glory due God's name connected with Israel's restoration. This can be seen in Psalm 106:47, "Save us, O LORD our God, and gather us from among the Gentiles, to give thanks to Your holy name."

THE NATIONS AND THE NAME

The nations mock God. In the light of Israel's degradation the psalmist asked, "Will the enemy blaspheme Your name forever?…Remember this, that the enemy has reproached, O LORD, and that a foolish people has blasphemed Your name" (Ps. 74:10, 18). When Israel is restored, God's name will be hallowed.

In Psalm 79 we read that God's name is ignored by the nations. This will lead to God's wrath upon them. That wrath will be the means of restoration and blessing for Israel, and God's name will be exalted (vv. 6, 9, 13). (See also Psalm 83:16, 18.)

Isaiah 64:1–4 contains a classic cry for God's revelation, judgment and intervention. For what purpose? To make His name known to the nations.

God's name is destined to be praised internationally (Ps. 86:9). The establishment of His kingdom is united to the universal praise of God's name (Isa. 24:20–25:1)!

NOW AND FOREVERMORE

Now, through Messiah, the remnants of the nations and the remnant of Israel praise the name of the Lord (Rom. 15:9). Ultimately all nations will hallow His name because God's righteous acts will be revealed (Rev. 15:4).

BECOMING GOD'S WATCHMEN

How then should we pray for Israel? First we must recognize that, apart from the remnant, Israel is under judicial blindness (Rom. 11:7, 25; 2 Cor. 3:14; 4:4). We are to intercede on their behalf, because Israel's watchmen are blind (Isa. 56:7, 10). In King David's time Israel was decimated by the judgment of God. The plague halted due to costly intercession (2 Sam. 24:25). In the same way that plague was stopped, the judicial blindness can be lifted as a result of costly intercession.

What does costly intercession look like?

In Isaiah 61:10–62:2 God established unceasing praise for His purposes. In Isaiah 62:6–7 unceasing prayer for the fulfillment of those purposes was enjoined. Those who intercede are God's watchmen.

Who are these watchmen? They are those who have a burden for the name of God to be hallowed. They are the New Covenant priests from all nations.

The content of their intercession is found in Psalm 122:6: "Pray for the peace of Jerusalem." With Paul, they agonize in prayer for Israel's salvation (Rom. 10:1).

The New Covenant Priesthood is a fellowship of those who bless God and bless others in His name. In Genesis 12:3 we read that those who "bless" Israel will in turn be blessed. According to God's Word we can bless Israel with God's presence (Num. 6:24). According to that same Word we will be blessed if we do.

SEEKING FIRST THE KINGDOM

God's name will not be ultimately hallowed "on earth as it is in heaven" until His kingdom is established over Israel and the nations. Those of us who have tasted the goodness of that reign should pray for Israel's restoration.

Jesus taught His disciples to pray for the hallowing of God's name. He was teaching them to pray for God's restorative purposes to be established among the house of Israel. God answers prayer. These purposes will be fulfilled, and His kingdom will come.

How should we pray for Israel in the End Times? Jesus said, "When you pray, say…

> "Our Father in heaven, for the sake of Your name restore Israel to Your purposes so that Your name may be sanctified in every way in all the earth. Let Your kingdom come; send Messiah to rule from Jerusalem so that Your will may be done on earth as it is in heaven."

Four

"Thy Kingdom Come"

Prayer Element—Intercession

Let Your Kingdom Come

Nations rise and nations fall
Leaders come and go
But Christ our King rules over all
And You will reign forever
Governments and dynasties boast
Of strength and power
But You alone reign sovereignly
And You will reign forever
Our God reigns forever

CHORUS
Let Your kingdom come
Let Your will be done
Let Your kingdom come
(Repeat)

Kings and queens leave legacies
Of temporary fame
Your throne remains eternally
You will reign forever
Our God reigns forever

(Repeat chorus)

One God one Lord one King one Majesty
One High one Lifted Up, one Holy Power

Our God reigns forever (repeat)
Our God reigns
Forever

Although the "kingdom of God" was not a highly developed theological concept in the Old Testament, there were concepts and events that laid the groundwork for its development. For example, God revealed Himself as a great king. In the Book of Exodus, God takes on the pharaoh of Egypt in order to spread His fame throughout the nations as a king. He entered into a covenant with His people as ancient kings always did. He then occupied a new land for His people and led them into battle, overthrowing the nations occupying that land. Much later, God chose a human king who was a man after His own heart. David's monarchy foreshadowed the promised coming and reign of God's chosen Messiah. The kingdom of David's son Solomon also prophetically foreshadowed the coming Messiah's reign. Like Solomon, the Messiah would be the kingly son of David.

During and after the Babylonian captivity, the prophets began to speak more specifically about the dramatic coming kingdom of the Messiah. Theological seed thoughts were planted in the hearts and minds of the Jewish nation, evoking a future hope of this divine kingdom come to earth. Interestingly, it was the intertestamental period of Jewish history and its literature that laid further important groundwork for the "kingdom theology" of the New Testament. This theological framework can also be referred to as "New Testament eschatology" (the study of the End Times)—for it has everything to do with a clash between this age, which is ending, and the future age, which has already begun.

BIBLICAL COSMOLOGY

Cosmology is the study of how the powers of the universe operate and interrelate. The Bible unveils the real story behind this fascinating subject. The cosmology of Jesus and the apostles was rooted in both the Old Testament and in many concepts of the Jewish people in the five-hundred-year period between the writing of the Old Testament and New Testament Scriptures.

A summary of the intertestamental kingdom of God cosmology might read as follows:

> Through the fall of man into sin, God has allowed a rival spiritual kingdom to exist upon the earth under the leadership of His ancient enemy, Satan, and his host of rebellious and fallen angels (demons). This evil empire has invaded this age and the nations of the world, and it now rules over and significantly dominates them. This evil kingdom is very real, well organized, malevolent and powerful—but it is inferior. It is the source of evil, sickness, suffering and death in the world. The kings of the earth and their religions and governments are pawns of Satan's kingdom.
>
> God does not, however, relinquish His ultimate and greater authority over Satan's kingdom or the nations. He never has, and He never will. God is "playing chess" with His inferior opponent, and He has prophesied His coming devastating victory. "Checkmate" will come suddenly and swiftly, after a carefully planned and steadily progressive strategy is executed, as the kingdom of God rushes in to bring both salvation and justice (judgment) to the nations. The people of God are instructed to wait expectantly and prayerfully for Messiah's kingdom. Meanwhile, they must remain faithful to the living God and His Word in the midst of their suffering.

Jesus and the apostles understood and validated this developing theological framework and language of spiritual warfare between the two rival kingdoms. This world-view is taken for granted in the New Testament Scriptures.

One important implication of all this is that God intended our understanding of His kingdom and the spiritual war that has been raging in this age also to be progressive. The theology of the kingdom of God is dynamic and unfolding in nature. Many of God's plans and much spiritual activity were not in plain theological view in the Old Testament. As the New Testament opens, a curtain is pulled back, and we get to see more clearly the "scene behind and above the scene."

Many of the paradoxical elements in New Testament theology can been observed in and around statements concerning the kingdom of God. If we do not embrace these paradoxes, we force ourselves into unnecessary and unfortunate polemical positions. In other words, we turn "both/and" issues into "either/or" issues, and we lose our theological, and therefore our relational and personal, balance.

MYSTERIES OF THE KINGDOM

Many aspects of God's truth are rooted in mystery and paradox—the Trinity and unity of God, the interplay between God's sovereignty and our freedom, our fallenness and dignity, God's goodness and the reality of evil, God's kindness and severity and the divine yet human nature of Jesus Christ, just to name a few. Although we often struggle with such concepts on a philosophical and intellectual level, we are actually designed to hold such mystery in our hearts. We are wondrously and strangely inspired when the mystery of God touches our spirits. Mystery messes with us—but in a good way! We are instinctively aware of our finiteness and of the infinity of our Creator. We know that we cannot now possibly know everything about Him and His ways. This dynamic reinforces to us that we are not omniscient and that we need to connect personally with the One who is. It helps us to relinquish a wrong control over our lives, other people and our circumstances. This is all by God's wise design. His greater intention in this matter of mystery is to bring us to a place of extreme awe, passionate worship and passionate prayer:

> Oh, the depth of the riches both of the wisdom and knowledge of God! How unsearchable are His judgments and His ways past finding out! "For who has known the

mind of the LORD? Or who has become His counselor? Or who has first given to Him and it shall be repaid to him?" For of Him and through Him and to Him are all things, to whom be glory forever. Amen.

—ROMANS 11:33–36

It is comforting to realize that the Scriptures teach us to expect this "run in" with our human limitations as we interface with truths about such a God as our God.

If we do not embrace the reality of mystery and paradox in our theology, then we will be confused and disoriented in our spiritual lives. We will never discover a proper rhythm in our walk with the Triune God. We will find ourselves living stiff, starchy, dispassionate and robotic lives—always angered and buffeted by God's commitment to break out of the carefully constructed boxes in which we have attempted to confine Him.

He said to them, "To you it has been given to know the mystery of the kingdom of God."

—MARK 4:11

Following are just four of the tensions related to the kingdom of God that we must come to embrace in our theology.

- The kingdom of God has both sudden and gradual dynamics.

    For as the lightning comes from the east and flashes to the west, so also will the coming of the Son of Man be.

    —MATTHEW 24:27

    Another parable He spoke to them: "The kingdom of heaven is like leaven, which a woman took and hid in three measures of meal till it was all leavened."

    —MATTHEW 13:33

- The kingdom has both passive and aggressive dimensions.

John answered and said, "A man can receive nothing unless it has been given to him from heaven."

—JOHN 3:27

And from the days of John the Baptist until now the kingdom of heaven suffers violence, and the violent take it by force. [I understand this verse to mean that since the beginning of John's ministry, God's people were given a fresh, divine commission to exercise the authority and power of God with a kind of holy violence (not by taking up literal arms) that has the capacity to plunder the kingdom of Satan for the glory of God and to rescue people who have been held captive by this evil foe.]

—MATTHEW 11:12

• The kingdom is both manifested and hidden.

As you go, preach this message: "The kingdom of heaven is near." Heal the sick, raise the dead, cleanse those who have leprosy, drive out demons. Freely you have received, freely give.

—MATTHEW 10:7–8, NIV

Once, having been asked by the Pharisees when the kingdom of God would come, Jesus replied, "The kingdom of God does not come with your careful observation, nor will people say, 'Here it is,' or 'There it is,' because the kingdom of God is within you."

—LUKE 17:20–21, NIV

• The kingdom of God is both present and future.

From that time Jesus began to preach and to say, "Repent, for the kingdom of heaven is at hand."

—MATTHEW 4:17

I charge you therefore before God and the Lord Jesus Christ, who will judge the living and the dead at His appearing and His kingdom.

—2 TIMOTHY 4:1

ALREADY AND NOT YET

It is this fourth paradox to which we now turn our attention. This "present evil age" (Gal. 1:4) is under the power of the evil one (1 John 5:19) and is destined for divine judgment and destruction (2 Pet. 3:7). The full judgment on this age is being delayed only because God is patiently longing for the people of the earth to come to repentance and be saved from eternal damnation. The kingdom of God was prefigured by certain Old Testament events including the Exodus, the possessing of Canaan, the reigns of King David and King Solomon and the building and later restoration of the temple.

However, something mysteriously wonderful did interrupt and forever disrupt the demonic powers that have ruled over this age. With the Incarnation and all of the events that surrounded the first coming of Jesus and His death, resurrection and ascension, the power of the future age—the kingdom of God—was visited upon this evil age.

PRAYERFACT 7

—Prayerfact 6 (see page 64)

God's eternal life is related to and inseparable from His love, for "God is love" in His very essence. Therefore, God invites us (in contrast to forcing us) to share and then bear, not just our own human love, but also His divine love, in and through our lives, relationships, work and through our faculties of spirit, mind, will, emotion and body.

—Prayerfact 8 (see page 87)

God Himself invaded this fallen world in the Person of Jesus the Messiah and inaugurated the "kingdom of God." The "end" showed up "ahead of time" in the Person and ministry of Jesus Christ. (See Hebrews 1:2; 9:26; 1 Corinthians 10:11; James 5:8–9; 1 Peter 4:7; 1 John 2:18; Revelation. 1:8.)

The kingdom of God is really here, only not *fully* here. It is *already* and *not yet.* The future age has come upon and now overlaps with the present age. This has created a tension and an intensified warfare between the forces of righteousness and wickedness. Satan and his kingdom were defeated and judged at the cross. He was stripped of his legal claim of authority over the nations of men. Yet he has been allowed to continue his activity in this age—although with a mortal wound. In fact, the wound enrages him, and he is seeking to take as many people to hell with him as possible before his time runs out.

OUR PART IN THE KINGDOM

Christians—the "sons of the kingdom"—now live in the challenge of this spiritual/moral tension. This earth is our proving ground and our training base for the glorious functions we will occupy in the age to come. It is a good fight. God has arranged this environment for our good, allowing us to participate in His kingdom as His coworkers. We are permitted the challenge and dignity of becoming overcomers through the powerful work of Jesus Christ on our behalf.

It is granted to us to taste of the powers of the age to come here and now (Heb. 6:5). We have received a significant down payment of our full inheritance through the Holy Spirit's ministry within and among us. A transcendent life in Messiah has now become possible for the people of God in this world (John 16:33; Rom. 8:1–4). In our excitement and longing for the Second Coming of Jesus, we have often undermined the awesome power of His first coming and the power that flows from it into the church—the potential to effectively disciple multiplied millions of people for the glory of God.

By viewing the kingdom of God through the lens of New Testament eschatology, we can understand the philosophical framework out of which many, if not most, major New Testament doctrines flow. The doctrines of the work of Christ, the Holy Spirit, the Church, world missions and even sanctification—which is often pictured as a battle between the old and new creations—are significantly informed by this framework.

"SIT AT MY RIGHT HAND"

The LORD said to my Lord, "Sit at My right hand, till I

make Your enemies Your footstool." The LORD shall send
the rod of Your strength out of Zion. Rule in the midst of
Your enemies! Your people shall be volunteers in the day
of Your power; in the beauties of holiness, from the
womb of the morning, you have the dew of Your youth.

—PSALM 110:1–3

Psalm 110 is the most important Old Testament prophecy for
kingdom theology. It is by far the most quoted and referred to
Old Testament passage of Scripture in the New Testament. It is
indisputable that this picture of the Messiah reigning at the
Lord's right hand was fulfilled through the resurrection and
ascension of Jesus. (See Mark 16:19–20; Acts 2:30–39; 5:31;
Ephesians 1:20–23; Hebrews 1:3; 10:12–13.) Jesus is not waiting to become king; He is king already! He is ruling in the
midst of His enemies, who have not quite yet figured out who
is in control. The kingdom is alive and well on Planet Earth.
The devil is also alive—but not so well! His kingdom is experiencing violent death throes. This will become more clear as
the very end approaches.

This scenario is truly astounding! Jesus Christ already has all
authority in heaven and on earth, and He is living out His rule
through—not apart from—His redeemed people. No matter
how poorly the church may have done from time to time
through the centuries, it is certain that before this age wraps up,
God is going to capture and subdue the hearts of Christians in
the love of Jesus. The Lord is going to bare His holy arm and
flex His muscles in the sight of all the nations before it's over.
This understanding imparts to us a realistic optimism based in
prophetic Scriptures regarding the success of our mission in
this age. The Spirit-filled church is the primary agent of the
kingdom of God and is extending the reign of Christ by proclaiming and demonstrating the gospel of the kingdom of God.
We know from Scripture that not all will come to faith. But we
do have a biblical hope for a massive international ingathering
of people coming to Jesus before the coming of the great and

terrible day of the Lord (Rev. 7:9–17; Acts 2:17–21).

What are the implications of kingdom theology for the last days and the final generation of believers? The Scripture teaches us that during the last days, a divine melodrama of unprecedented proportions will unfold. Rather than God vs. the Egyptian pharaoh on a local stage, this drama will feature God vs. an international antichrist on a global stage. Rather than one hundred twenty receiving the fire of God in a Jerusalem upper room, the Spirit will be poured out internationally on all flesh—on men and women, on the old and the young. The last day's spiritual equation will be *(Exodus + Acts) to the second power!* Judgment and salvation will come to a crescendo on the earth in fulfillment of numerous ancient prophecies.

KINGDOM CONSCIOUSNESS

In a real sense, it does not matter to what degree these glorious and terrible things are fulfilled in our generation. We are already living in the kingdom, and the eager expectation of His return is to beat continually in our hearts. God will not chide us if we pray in faith for the great global revival and the release of the last days' ministry of the church, and yet die before it occurs. Christians have already crossed over the *big gap* in human experience. It is not our coming physical death.

> **PRAYERFACT #8**
>
> —Prayerfact 7 (see page 84)
>
> *Through Jesus and by the Holy Spirit, God has reached down to humanity and made a way for a personal connection to be made with Him on the basis of our receiving it as a free gift.*
>
> —Prayerfact 9 (see page 98)

Rather, it is our present deliverance from a "living death" in sin into eternal life in the Spirit of God. *For true believers the line between this life and the next is almost blurred.* The early Christians understood this, and therefore they practically welcomed martyrdom. The heroes of faith referred to in Hebrews

11 also understood, and they lived with a kingdom-of-God consciousness that informed and directed their earthly walk. This is how we also ought to live.

The phrase that Jesus taught us to pray, "Your kingdom come," was spoken in an emphatic tense—"Come, Your kingdom!" This implies that God is calling us to boldly call on His power to manifest among us here and now. Just as Jacob of old wrestled with God and would not let Him go until He blessed him, so God respects and even enjoys our "wrestling" with Him in prayer. He wants us to fervently call for the demonstration of the Spirit's power to counter the evils in our world. God has strategically designed this prayer dynamic for our growth in the Spirit.

This is one of the primary ways that we are being prepared for our function in the age to come, when we will rule and reign with Christ Jesus over all other things. We must pray for the Holy Spirit to come and break through those things that are resisting the application of God's kingdom in this age. He will do this very thing for which we ask—again and again—if we persevere in faith and obedience. Let us not easily or quickly take "no" for an answer. It is God's will that we, through prayer, labor to see His permissive will yield to His perfect will in many ways and in many situations. As difficult as it is for some people to appreciate, God really does like this kind of humble and holy boldness on the part of His children!

1. List all the various spheres of your life and pray for God to extend His rule and reign into those arenas. Ask Him to give you a vision of what your life would look like and how it would function if Jesus' lordship would be fully demonstrated within and through you. Regularly pray for God's kingdom and Spirit to come into those same realms and regions of the lives of your family members, friends and neighbors.

2. Contemplate your approaching physical death and standing before Jesus Christ face to face. What do you think He will ask you about your earthly life? What would you like to be able to say to Him on that day?

3. Meditate on Colossians 3:22–25. Consider how you would work or study if the Lord were your boss or school teacher, and then really work and study this week as if He were. Try to make the emotional connection to the fact that you are going to be rewarded in eternity for being faithful in your earthly responsibilities, even though they often seem mundane.

Father in heaven, I thank You for Your kingdom that is available and accessible here and now. I receive it even as I pray. You have already set Your King upon Your holy hill. Christ Jesus, You are King of all the kings of the earth! Father, I joyfully anticipate the consummation of this age and the full manifestation of Your Son's kingdom. Until then, let the power and grace of the age to come break through the dark canopy of evil that envelops this world.

Pierce the darkness again and again with Your heavenly light. Come, kingdom of God! Come, Holy Spirit! Cause Your whole Church—every true believer in Christ—to live in the fullness of the Holy Spirit. Let the Church be the Church. Allow Your Word and Spirit to be dominant over our lives. Put the unbelief of this world to shame, and beautify the lives of all who live under Your gracious reign. Let every area of human existence be affected and instructed by the presence of Your heavenly kingdom here on earth.

I pray for an unprecedented outpouring of Your Spirit upon the nations in this hour of human history. Send a global revival, and let Your glory be upon us throughout every nation even as gross darkness covers the earth and Satan displays his final rages. Let us, Your children, shine as lights and simply hold forth Your Word of truth in this wicked and perverse world. Give this generation of believers a "forerunner spirit" and a prophetic anointing that will prepare Your way and complete the Great Commission You have given us. Release the deep rivers of holy passion from our hearts to combat and overcome the evil lust of this age—even unto death. Let the Spirit and the Bride say, "Come." Amen.

Prayer for spiritual gifts

I thank my God always concerning you for the grace of God which was given to you by Christ Jesus, that you were enriched in everything by Him in all utterance and all knowledge, even as the testimony of Christ was confirmed in you, so that you come short in no gift, eagerly waiting for the revelation of our Lord Jesus Christ, who will also confirm you to the end, that you may be blameless in the day of our Lord Jesus Christ.

— 1 CORINTHIANS 1:4–8

Prayer for grace for believers

The grace of our Lord Jesus Christ be with you.

— 1 CORINTHIANS 16:23

Prayer for financial provision and abundance

Now may He who supplies seed to the sower, and bread for food, supply and multiply the seed you have sown and increase the fruits of your righteousness, while you are enriched in everything for all liberality, which causes thanksgiving through us to God.

— 2 CORINTHIANS 9:10–11

Prayer for honorable living

Now I pray to God that you do no evil, not that we should appear approved, but that you should do what is honorable, though we may seem disqualified.

— 2 CORINTHIANS 13:7

Five

"Thy Will Be Done in Earth, As It Is in Heaven"

Prayer Element—Intercession

Fill the Earth

Spirit of God receive our prayer
Pour out Your Spirit everywhere
Let Jesus boldly be proclaimed
And every heart confess His name
We cry for mercy on the land
Let righteousness prevail again
Redeem the standard of Your will
May Your desires be fulfilled
We appeal before Your throne
Let Messiah's name be known

CHORUS
Fill the earth with Your glory Lord
Fill the world with the revelation of Your Son

We ask for holiness and grace
To be raised up in every place
For every nation every tongue
To bow before the Chosen One
With one voice one holy aim
Free the world in Jesus' name

(Repeat chorus 2 times)

God delegated to Adam and Eve authority over the world in the beginning. They were appointed as God's vice-rulers over the earth. It seems that God's original intention was that Adam and Eve would eventually "export" Paradise to the whole planet. However, when they failed the moral test set before them and chose a life of independence from God, they actually obeyed Satan. As a result, Satan's evil counter-kingdom usurped mastery over humanity, and Satan became "the god of this world" (2 Cor. 4:4, NAS). He has an invisible intelligence network of disembodied spirits who do his bidding and seek to keep humanity in spiritual deception. Some of the lower orders of evil spirits actually inhabit people and places, seeking to drive humanity into all kinds of evil things. The higher, more powerful ranks work to keep whole cities, regions and nations in bondage to deception and turmoil. (See Ephesians 6.)

When Satan became the god of this world, the world became a fallen place and humankind a fallen race. God had forewarned our first parents about the curse of death that would be effected by their rebellion. Death takes on many forms, but the harsh reality of physical death that confronts us all is a clear proof of the reality of the serious consequences of the Fall of man in the Garden.

THE EARTH AND THE WORLD

In the New Testament, "the world" is typically referred to as lying under the power of the devil and his fallen angels (1 John 5:19). We are in an evil age that is under the judgment of God (Gal. 1:4). Theologically speaking, the *earth* should be distinguished clearly from the *world*. God commands us not to "love the world or the things in the world" (1 John 2:15). Whoever is a "friend of the world" makes herself/himself a spiritual adulterer and an enemy of God (James 4:4). When the Bible states that "God so loved the world" (John 3:16), Jesus was referring to the fact that God loves and cares for the *people* of the world. However, He does not love the systems of government, religion and education. He does not agree with "worldly" attitudes and styles of interpersonal relationships, or the lifestyles, priorities and values people have generally chosen for themselves. In fact, God hates most of these things. The things men esteem, God often despises, and things that God despises, men highly esteem (Luke 16:15). The Bible pictures the peoples and societies of the world as having organized themselves against God and His kingdom and having been deceived and manipulated by the kingdom of darkness (Ps. 2; 1 Cor. 2:8). Through the centuries, our ways have perpetrated and perpetuated sinful pride, greed, hatred, lust, excessive physical indulgences and wars. All of these ways of humanity have been and will be judged justly by God for the evil they manifest. So much for "the world." What about "the earth?"

> **PRAYERFACT 9**
>
> —Prayerfact 8 (see page 87)
>
> *Our part in becoming a child of God is to receive voluntarily the gift of eternal life by believing what God has spoken and promised us in Jesus Christ—who He is and what He has done.*
>
> —Prayerfact 10 (see page 103)

"The earth is the LORD'S, and all its fullness" (Ps. 24:1). The earth belongs to God, and He has always cared about it. When He created it along with all of the visible creation, He called it "very good" (Gen. 1:31). God will one day renovate the earth, and it will reflect a degree of God's glory and perfection that it never has before (2 Pet. 3:13). In fact, the renewed earth will be the future residence and resting place of the heavenly city of God (Rev. 21:1–3).

God has never abdicated His lordship over the earth. He is the true and rightful King of both the heavens and the earth (Acts 17:24). The rulers of the world, though, haven't figured out yet who actually is in ultimate control. There is a day of reckoning quickly approaching. The world will not end until God clearly reveals the lordship of Jesus Christ over the kingdoms of this world. This He will do at just the right time and place in human history. Christ has already been crowned King of the kingdoms of the whole earth, but His reign has not yet been expressed fully in a visible and obvious way in the eyes of most of humanity (Rev. 1:5; 1 Cor. 15:24–26).

Through the centuries, the mission of the Church—those called out of the worldly system of sin and rebellion—has been to persuade as many people as possible concerning the good news of Jesus and His rightful claim of lordship over all the people groups of this world. Those who heed the message will be saved from the wrath of God against sin. They will be forgiven and adopted into God's family through their faith in the merits of Christ's death, resurrection and ascension on their behalf. If they reject the message of Christ, they will stand before the infinitely holy and just God with nothing and no one to compensate for the sins that they have committed against God and others. They will bear the just punishment for rejecting God's offer of salvation through faith in Jesus: They will be banished forever from His presence to a place of unimaginable regret and torment (2 Thess. 1:6–10).

GOD'S CARE FOR THE EARTH

Because God cares deeply about this earth, Jesus taught us to pray for the will of God to break through the spiritual and moral darkness that blankets this planet. We must pray for His will to be established both "on earth" and "in earth"—that is, in literal human beings who have been formed from the earth's dust. Through believers in Christ who know and do the will of God, God wants to set before the people of this world a credible and visible witness of His reality and His ways. When we are praying for the will of God on the earth, we are asking God to manifest the "Jesus way" of living earthly life in contrast to the "worldly way."

What does the way of Christ look like for marriages, for

education and for the nurture of children? What does it mean for stewarding finances, for conducting business, for governing nations, for worshiping and seeking after God? How is He honored in the way we punish crime, use natural resources, help the poor and the sick, manage our physical bodies and drives, express our artistic, recreational and literary talents? Every kind of activity ordained by our Creator for human existence should reflect the wisdom of God's genius and the beauty of His grace. In all arenas of life God wants His will to be done on earth for the glory of Christ Jesus. The more excellently and faithfully God's people demonstrate and reflect God's wisdom and love in these practical ways, the better chance there will be for non-Christians to come to faith in Jesus. Moreover, loving God and wisely winning people to Christ is the proper motivation for whatever else God may have us do. And for this we should never apologize or be ashamed. This vision of God's kingdom touching every aspect of earthly life gives us plenty of specifics to pray about.

IS GOD'S WILL BEING DONE?

The Lord is a God who makes choices, who purposes and plans, who thinks and speaks, who is intentional in His actions. This is in part what is meant when theologians say that God is a "Person." He is a Person with perfect and infinite powers of volition. To possess a will has to do with the power of the mind to decide and do—the ability to strategize, determine and to carry out that determination. Our powers of will and volition are simply a finite and limited expression of this aspect of the image of God that is stamped upon our human soul. However, our will, like every other aspect of our being, has been touched and tainted by original sin—the sinful nature passed down to us via the moral fall of our first parents. The image of God in humans is still present, but every part of our being has been touched, tarnished and twisted by sin

We should celebrate and take great comfort in the fact that God has a will in relation to all things at all times, and that His will is the highest good for the whole universe. God's heart and mind are infinite in their capacities. Paul called God's will "that good and acceptable and perfect will of God" (Romans 12:2). We really wouldn't be inspired to worship with passion a lesser God.

Not only does God possess a perfect will, but we are called to perceive His will and then to surrender our wills to His. That is why the apostle Paul prayed for the believers at Colosse to be filled with the knowledge of His will in all wisdom and spiritual understanding (Col. 1:9). To discover the will of God for our lives and to do it are vital keys to an intimate relationship with Jesus—"Whoever does the will of My Father in heaven is My brother and sister and mother" (Matt. 12:50). To know the will of God and to do it is what makes our personal life (though not our body) indestructible despite whatever may happen to us circumstantially speaking—"and the world is passing away, and lust of it; but he who does the will of God abides forever" (1 John 2:17).

This leads us to a rather startling and sobering fact: The will of God is not being done, generally speaking, on this earth as it is in the heavens. Of course, this is the very reason Jesus instructs us to pray that it will be. "The whole world lies under the sway of the wicked one . . . for all that is in the world . . . is not from the Father, but is from the world" (1 John 5:19; 2:16). The wills of Satan and fallen humans are constantly being exercised and expressed on this earth.

Does this mean that God is neither omniscient nor omnipotent, as some Christians have been tempted to think? Obviously not, for the Scripture everywhere informs us that He is both. God's will is also being done in many ways and through many means right in the midst of the disobedience and rebellion of His fallen creatures. So why would a loving, holy, all-knowing and all-powerful God not enforce His will at all times throughout the entire universe? Simply put, *it has pleased Him to make room for other beings also to possess wills of their own and to grant them the freedom to exercise their wills.* This implies that God has lovingly and wisely chosen to make Himself and the whole creation *vulnerable* to the sorrow and pain that have come both from fallen angels and humans deviating from doing His perfect will.

As we hold the truths of God's sovereignty and the free choice of created beings together in philosophical tension, we conclude that God must have a *permissive will* in addition to His *perfect will.* He allows the things to take place that actually do, but He doesn't always cause or will them to be done. If this were not the case, then there would be no biblical references to the patience or tolerance of God—attributes of His character that are often celebrated in the Scriptures. People only have to be tolerant of things that they would prefer to be different than they are.

God "works all things according to the counsel of His will" (Eph. 1:11), but He has to "work" them. He "causes all things to work together for good to those who love God" (Rom. 8:28, NAS), but He must patiently "work them together" over time to cause this to occur in such a way that other wills are not violated. Only God is wise enough and great enough to be able to take imperfect and even bad people and situations and then patiently re-cast and incorporate them into His overall master plan for good. This reality certainly gives us good subjects and themes for our life of prayer!

THE NATURE OF LOVE

Why would God allow all of these complicating factors to exist in His universe? This can only be understood and appreciated in light of the voluntary nature of God's love. He has given us the dignity and liberty to choose whether or not we will live apart from believing in and loving Him. True love cannot be forced, and God Himself, who is love, will not violate this reality. He does not want an obedient race of automatons. Rather, He desires to have a voluntary army of humans who serve Him out of intelligent love and devotion that acknowledge His worth. *God would rather have the hearty and sincere love of imperfect friends than the passionless, enforced obedience of robots.* He is not and never has been short on power; rather He is short on voluntary human partners (Isa. 50:1–3). However, God has made it possible, through Jesus Christ and the power of the Holy Spirit, for us to embrace both the challenge and the invitation of this partnership.

DOING GOD'S WILL

Jesus had the right attitude toward His Father's will. As God has revealed His will by His Word, Jesus, the living Word of God, modeled to us the kind of attitude we should have toward our will and the will of God. He said He could rightly discern and righteously judge all things because He didn't seek His own will, but the will of His Father (John 6:38). Jesus possessed a human will, but He succeeded in continually yielding His will in order to do the Father's will. He had to wrestle with heavy temptations and spiritual

> ## PRAYERFACT 10
>
> —Prayerfact 9 (see page 98)
>
> *The dynamic connection between God and us is purposely based on God's integrity, honor and love rather than on our ability to earn God's favor or acceptance. This is so that we will not destroy others or ourselves by the arrogance that a sense of earning God's favor would generate in our hearts.*
>
> —Prayerfact 11 (see page 115)

forces of darkness to accomplish this, but He was victorious in every such battle. He also told us that if we would "[will] to do His will" (John 7:17), we also would possess great spiritual discernment. Truth is more frequently found on the other side of a *moral* test than of an *intellectual* one.

Finally, we have the marvelous promise in the New Testament that God will actually strengthen our weak wills by the power of Christ's Spirit (Phil. 2:13; 4:13). God is actually at work within us to realign our wills so that we desire to surrender to His higher will. He hasn't left us to ourselves in our weakness, but the things He has commanded He has also promised to help us carry out. We simply need to admit our weakness, call on Him for help and rearrange our lives so that we feed daily on the simple and doable things that God has said will nourish our souls. He draws us into these ways of life by offering us the superior pleasures of godliness in contrast to the passing pleasures of sin. As we delight ourselves in the Lord, He gives us the desires of our hearts (Ps. 37:4). In the very process of our falling in love with the most adorable Person in the universe, the Spirit of God fills our hearts with joy, purges inferior desires and lusts from our souls, imparts new desires that are in line with His and then fulfills *those* desires within us over the course of time.

As we boldly intercede for the will of God to be done on earth as it is in the heavens, He is standing by longing to accomplish His will by His Spirit. He grants human beings the desire and power to accomplish His will through the great and marvelous promises He has made to provide for us through faith in Jesus Christ. Specifically, He provides "all things that pertain to life and godliness," empowering us to "[escape] the corruption that is in the world" by the presence of evil desires (2 Pet. 1:3–4). The deal He has made is very hard to refuse when we understand it rightly. Every excuse and argument against it has been anticipated and then trumped by God. We simply have no good reason to avoid doing the will of God.

JESUS' LAST WILL AND TESTAMENT

In many cultures, people prepare their "last will and testament." This is typically a written document that expresses the wishes of one who has died for the proper use of the resources she or he has left behind.

God has also prepared His last will and testament. The Book of Hebrews uses this word picture to give us insight into the importance and nature of God's will. His will, in this sense, revolves around Jesus Christ and is inseparable from Jesus' life, death, resurrection and ascension. Jesus inaugurated the New

Covenant (testament) through His substitutionary death. This New Covenant is perfect, faultless and therefore final. It also follows that this will or covenant was to be written down. This will is expressed in what has become the New Testament portion of the Bible.

Like the written wills of our day, God has also written out His will. (See Hebrews 9:16–17; 10:7–10.) The Holy Scriptures contain the written and ratified will of God. The "testator," Jesus Christ, has died to reinforce to us its relevancy and power. In order for the will of God to be done *on* earth, it must be done *in* the earth. That is, it must be done by human beings, who are called "earthen vessels" (2 Cor. 4:7). True Christianity is incarnational by nature; it is to be "fleshed out" by people who actually do the will of God out of a motivation of love and gratitude. This will of God will not and cannot be done apart from believing and obeying the Word of God. We must therefore become intimately acquainted with the Holy Scripture, which gives us the wisdom and motivation to know and do our Father's will. Christ has provided for us all the resources that we need to ensure that His legacy will be carried on by us and spread abroad to all the earth through the power of the Holy Spirit who has been given to us.

1. Go somewhere to get all alone for a whole day. Write down all the deepest desires of your heart that you want see come about in your life. Then ask God if each one of these desires is His highest will for your life. Tell Him that you want His will to prevail over any misguided desires you may have, and then lay them down before Him.

2. Recognize something going on in the life of a friend or family member that you really believe is not the will of God; pray about it as long as you need to until it changes for the better.

3. Serve God by doing something practical and visible to beautify the environment around your neighborhood or workplace.

Father in heaven, thank You for this earth. You created it and fashioned it for Your pleasure. You called it good in the very beginning. Even under the weight of its many sins, it still reflects so much of Your beauty and genius. Thank You that You have many plans for this earth and that even in the age to come it will be renewed and fully restored. The earth will become what it has never yet been. Even now the whole earth is full of Your glory. May Your glory and the knowledge of it cover the earth as the waters cover the sea.

Remind me of the marvels of light and motion, the immense power of the seas, the majesty of the mountains, the hidden life in seeds, the privilege of reproduction, the miracle of the human body, the joys of marriage, family, friendship and noble work and the amazing accomplishments of humanity. By Your power and Spirit, may the powers of heaven bend down to kiss this planet again and again. I praise You for the life that You have given humans to live on earth. Give the peoples of this world a revolutionary revelation of what we can become and do when we offer up the natural life You have given to us to interface with the eternal life You offer us in Jesus Christ.

Father, I praise You that You have a will for all things and that Your will is good, acceptable and perfect. I magnify Your power and ability to work all things after the counsel of Your will. Nothing can ultimately prevail over Your will for this universe. Thank You that the angelic hosts of highest heaven do Your bidding without question or debate. Your will is most worthy to be served and carried out.

I grieve over the fact that Your will is so often left undone in the earth—even in and through my life. I praise You for the gift of my will. Why would You make Yourself so vulnerable? I have so often abused this gift of choice. Yet it has pleased You to give me a real life to live. Help me to honor You by living for Your glory. Strengthen me to bend my will until it is conformed to Yours. I confess that my purposes and plans are flawed and laced with error. I surrender my will to You again today. Let Your will be known. Let Your will be done. Let Your will prevail—in my life and in all the earth. In the name of Jesus I pray. Amen.

Prayer for maturity for believers

For we are glad when we are weak and you are strong. And this also we pray, that you may be made complete.

—2 CORINTHIANS 13:9

Prayer for grace, love and the Spirit's nearness

The grace of the Lord Jesus Christ, and the love of God, and the communion of the Holy Spirit be with you all. Amen.

—2 CORINTHIANS 13:14

Prayer for grace to the spirits of believers

Brethren, the grace of our Lord Jesus Christ be with your spirit. Amen.

—GALATIANS 6:18

Prayer for the spirit of wisdom and revelation

Therefore I also, after I heard of your faith in the Lord Jesus and your love for all the saints, do not cease to give thanks for you, making mention of you in my prayers: that the God of our Lord Jesus Christ, the Father of glory, may give to you the spirit of wisdom and revelation in the knowledge of Him, the eyes of your understanding being enlightened; that you may know what is the hope of His calling, what are the riches of the glory of His inheritance in the saints, and what is the exceeding greatness of His power toward us who believe, according to the working of His mighty power which He worked in Christ when He raised Him from the dead and seated Him at His right hand in the heavenly places, far above all principality and power and might and dominion, and every name that is named, not only in this age but also in that which is to come.

And He put all things under His feet, and gave Him to be head over all things to the church, which is His body, the fullness of Him who fills all in all.

—EPHESIANS 1:15–23

Six

"Give Us This Day Our Daily Bread"

Prayer Element—Personal Petition

O God

You bind up the brokenhearted
You set the captives free
You bring the light to pierce the darkness
And bring Your grace for all to see
Oh God Oh God

For those who mourn You pour out comfort
You provide for those who grieve
A crown of beauty instead of ashes
Your garment of praise covers me

O God Father God
O God Father God

You bring streams into the desert
And cause the harvest fields to grow
When You breathe life is abundant
You cause the rivers of life to flow

O God Father God
O God Father God

Give us this day our daily bread
O God our provider

In this section of the Lord's Prayer, Jesus is teaching us literally to pray for our daily physical and material needs to be met by our Father in heaven. For some people, this seems to be much too mundane and earthy to be the case. Their ideas about "true spirituality" must transcend such basic and practical bodily and material necessities. They are compelled to spiritualize the request for "bread" and make it refer to the spiritual "food" of truth, wisdom and such. However, anyone who has ever known true hunger would not be so tempted. Likewise, people who understand biblical spirituality know that the bodily and physical part of our lives is extremely important to God and to our life and growth in Christ.

God wants us to interact with Him and rely upon Him for the most simple and basic aspects of our lives. The Father in heaven loves for us to fellowship with Him in an ongoing dialogue regarding our daily activities, burdens, joys, needs and desires. Spend a whole day sometime talking to God and asking Him about every feeling, situation, person, need, desire, question, dilemma, disappointment, conversation, meal, task, issue, Bible verse, piece of news, daydream, fear, temptation, failure and anything else that you may experience or be exposed to that day. Listen for His leadings and responses. This is the very practical stuff of having a real friendship with God. Remember that He is omnipresent and has the capacities to simultaneously care about all things great and small. It's rather difficult for God to get overwhelmed!

Worry vs. Responsibility

Also woven into this instruction on prayer is Jesus' call to contentment and freedom from anxiety about the future. Too many human beings are simply fretting and striving to secure themselves and their possessions for an uncertain future. (See Psalm 37.) They live as though there has to be some way to remove this uncertainty factor. However, it is just a fantasy at the root level, and a dangerous one at that. Such foolishness drives millions of people into harmful, destructive and immoral ways of coping with life (1 Tim. 6:6–10).

In this prayer, Jesus is telling us to ask God today for the things we need today. If we are trusting God and seeking to do His will, then we're not to waste our spiritual, emotional or physical energies worrying about how we are going to survive physically in the future (Phil. 4:6–7). Of course, this is not a categorical condemnation denouncing working for, saving for or spending for something that will be useful to our lives beyond today. This kind of wisdom can represent the good stewardship of our earthly resources. God actually commands us in Scripture to work hard, earn our own bread, spend prudently, save wisely and invest shrewdly. This is a part of our responsibility before God (1 Tim. 5:8). However, we are not to allow our lives to be consumed with anxiety about the future or the pressure to hoard our God-given resources. Greed and avarice often seek to disguise themselves as wisdom.

The point is, the *exact details* regarding how any of us will physically survive in the future are *uncertain,* and we should never put our trust in material wealth or things as though they will make our earthly lives totally secure. Our only security is found in depending on the One who is much bigger than we are and serving His purposes.

We were never created to live our lives apart from fellowship with the living God. The insecurity and fear we naturally experience regarding our future is to be translated into daily dependence upon our great and good heavenly Father and His stated commitment to care for us in this life and the next. We are never to outgrow this dependency dynamic; it is the essence of walking by faith rather than by sight (2 Cor. 5:7). No matter how wiser or more responsible we become in God, we are still His little children, and we should delight in the positive qualities of being childlike before Him.

Children of good parents know their folks are going to take care of their needs. They know their parents would even sacrifice their lives for them if necessary. In relation to their parents, healthy children trust easily, receive warmly, ask without shame, know their limitations, express their emotions and affections openly, enjoy their parents' company and desire to please them. We could do with more of the childlikeness before our Father that Jesus calls us to: "Unless you are converted and become as little children, you will by no means enter the kingdom of heaven" (Matt. 18:3).

The apostle Paul spoke about the value of learning to be content in whatever material or financial situations God places us from season to season (Phil. 4:10–13). Indeed, most people go through various seasons in the financial arena—God sees to it! If we allow the grace of financial contentment to settle in our hearts, then we become a threat to the

PRAYERFACT 11

—Prayerfact 10 (see page 103)

To refuse the offer of interfacing with the higher life of God is the essence of the "pride of life" that is of this fallen age (the world).

—Prayerfact 12 (see page 118)

kingdom of darkness like never before, for we will not be able to be manipulated by the fear of lack or the love of money. Incidentally, there are multitudes of both rich and poor people who are in bondage to both! Through contentment, our souls will be liberated to focus upon the things that really matter in this life. God really isn't that concerned about whether we are rich or just have enough to make it from day to day.

God doesn't measure success by our earning power or the size of our bank account. Biblical success is essentially about allowing God to love us, loving Him in response and loving our neighbor as ourselves. God is primarily concerned with the state of our heart and how rich we are in the ways of love. Of course, it is His will that we work hard and live within our means—this is our responsibility. Finances typically have a way of just falling into place in our lives in every season when we put our pursuit of the kingdom of God first. There are sometimes exceptional situations in our lives in which we may need to rely on the help of others, but we will learn through this kind of weakness and vulnerability also. So will the people whom God calls to assist us. Usually we will be able to pass this blessing on to others in need after we come through such a trial. So many people are not enjoying their lives today. They are not living heartily for Christ because they are distracted and drained by the disorder of soul created by a lack of contentment and the very real presence of anxiety. Deliver us, O God!

THE IMPORTANCE OF ASKING

From one perspective, it seems rather strange that an omniscient and omnipotent God would ordain that we should ask Him to provide for us the basic things we need for physical survival. Doesn't He already know what we need? He obviously does (Matt. 6:32). In fact, doesn't He also know that we're going ask Him for something even before we do so? Psalm 139 states that He even knows this! For that matter, why would He require that we ask for anything, significant or otherwise?

Prayer is a mysterious event when you examine it philosophically. What is the use of taking the time and expending the energy to inform God of things He already knows? Aren't there more productive ways of using our personal resources and creative energies? Yet Jesus makes it clear that we *are* to ask our heavenly Father each day to provide for our physical necessities. "Bread" can be viewed as the food most representative of all food, drink and covering essential to life.

Apparently, our wise Father knows and values things that we, in our natural thinking, find difficult to grasp. The almighty God actually desires to enter into a genuine interactive friendship with us—unmighty as we are. Prayer is not a cruel cosmic game. It is a conversation that really matters both in the heavens and on the earth. The time, energy and activities needed to build a loving personal relationship with another are oftentimes contrary to our performance-oriented Western lives, which gravitate to pursuits yielding more tangible rewards.

We need to have a conversion of our heart values so that we will not be buffeted by false guilt if we sometimes sacrifice outward performance for the sake of experiencing more loving relationships. Certainly our relationship with God is the most important relationship we have, and even it is not based on our performance of duties. Our "performance" of righteousness flows out of loving friendship with God. When passionate love from and for God is at the base of our lives, good works will be a natural by-product. God is our *Father,* and He loves to hear our voice and respond to our stated needs. We must take the time and expend the energy to keep up our dialogue with Him.

THE IMPACT OF ANSWERED PRAYER

Many good things result from our asking God specifically and persistently for what we need. Jesus said, "Ask, and you will receive, that your joy may be full" (John 16:24). Our Father wants us to experience the delight of an intimate relationship with Him, one in which we regularly see Him answer our prayers. Pascal referred to the "dignity of causality" that God confers upon believers in Christ. We are actual partners, coworkers, with God in His kingdom. Through weeks, months and years of prayer, we develop a personal history of interacting with the living God as we witness His response to us. Through this spiritual dynamic, our confidence in His power to provide imparts a greater experiential authority to our witness to the reality of Jesus in this world.

Jesus also said, "And whatever you ask in My name, that I will do, that the Father may be glorified in the Son" (John 14:13). Our Father is the great and generous Provider of all good things to all humanity. When we make daily petition for the basic necessities of life, God is continually exalted in our eyes as the true Source of these provisions. This God-consciousness wards off ingratitude, spiritual blindness and a multitude of untold evils. The Father wants us to glorify Him as the awesome Provider of these blessings because in truth, we are the needy ones and He is the Provider (Acts 17:25–28). When we glorify God for who He actually is, our lives take on more of the beauty of His holiness and increasingly reflect the glory of His divine order.

PARENT/CHILD DYNAMICS OF PRAYER

We really are the children of God, and the dynamics of our relationship with Him are more similar to the relationship between earthly parents and their children than we might initially expect. We struggle with this because we all know that human parents don't have the same attributes and capacities as God. This, however, does not negate the similarities. For instance, parents love to provide for the children. Being a provider is not a burdensome drain upon a loving and resourceful parent. Rather, it is a deeply satisfying pleasure and honor. So it is with God and His children (Ps. 50:15).

Jesus said, "It is more blessed to give than to receive" (Acts 20:35). He, above all persons, seeks to experience this blessing (happiness). God Himself has set the example of the blessedness of giving for us to emulate. Of course, this also means that "receiving" is a blessing, otherwise "giving" would be evil! Therefore, God has ordained that we walk in the blessedness of receiving and also in the superblessedness of giving. This is truly an ingenious basis for both an economic and a relationship system. Just imagine what this world would be like if every person walked in the revelation of a cycle of life rooted in gratefully receiving and generously

---

PRAYERFACT 12

—Prayerfact 11 (see page 115)

We are all naturally prone to "independent living" due to the human pride passed down to us via the sin of our first parents.

—Prayerfact 13 (see page 135)

---

giving. It would be like heaven already is. Happiness is not a limited commodity in the universe; it is like a holy virus that can and should be spread. Christians, above all other people, should be good advertisements for this quality of happiness.

At times earthly parents "test the desire level" in their children regarding the things that they *say* they want so much. Wise parents do not always respond to their children's requests the first time the children ask. This would be a recipe for spoiling a weak and immature person. Sometimes good parents might put them off to make sure that they are serious, or they might require their children to save their own money to buy what they desire. This way it becomes worth more to the children when they finally get it. If parents will sometimes require their children to wait patiently for their desire to be fulfilled, then the answer, when it comes, will evoke a greater and longer lasting joy and gratitude in the children's hearts. So it is with God and His children (Luke 11:13).

There are other situations in which parents will not automatically provide something for their children until the children specifically ask for that thing. When the children speak up, and the desire is legitimate, loving parents quickly respond to the request without a trace of a begrudging or unwilling attitude. The children receive that for which they have asked, but they would have gone without it had they not asked. So it is with God and His children. "Ye have not, because ye ask not" (James 4:2, KJV). This has got to be one of the most profoundly amazing and convicting principles in all of Scripture.

Yet again, there are times when children's persistence ultimately prevails over any reluctance in the parents to grant a specific request. The parents see the passionate desire in their loved ones, and they simply cannot withhold the request. The parents will even rearrange other things to fit the answer to the request into their larger plans for their children's lives. The priorities of parents can potentially be altered by the expressed desire of their children. So it is sometimes with God and His children.

God's children at times prevail upon Him through persevering prayer (Luke 18:1–8). It is God's will that we prevail over His *permissive* will through prayer in order to see His *perfect* will established. This is significantly what prayer is about by its very nature—God truly listening to the voice of human beings and genuinely responding to them (Josh. 10:14). God likes that kind of bold "wrestling" in prayer—just as earthly fathers enjoy wrestling with their kids to affectionately bond with them and to help them develop their strength and agility. This is an amazing doctrine of Scripture that has been abused by many and ignored by most. It remains true nonetheless. Yet we can only experience the joy of prevailing prayer through deep intimacy with the Holy Spirit and a willingness to fully embrace the cross of Christ.

1. List ten prayers that God has answered in your past. Spend some time thanking Him for listening and responding to you. Then list ten things that you want God to do for you.

2. Give away some material possession(s) in which you have found some of your identity and security.

3. Fast from eating food for at least two meals, and then eat a simple meal thanking God for how He has provided for your needs.

Father, I come to You in the name of the Lord Jesus. Without shame I boldly ask You to give me the things I need for life today. Please forgive me for not speaking with You often and freely enough about the little matters of my life—I fear that this has somehow even kept me from trusting You with the bigger concerns of my life. I want it to be different from now on. I want to walk with You and talk with You along life's narrow way, just as the old song said. You are my awesome and gracious Father, and I know that You love me.

Your precious promises have granted to me all things pertaining to life and godliness. Preserve my life and give me abundance so that I have something to give away freely to others. I thank You for the promise that You will provide for my necessities this day and that You will do the same each day You have appointed for me to live on this earth. I praise You for the compassion and care that You have in Your heart for me as Your child. I ask for the breath, health, food, shelter, strength, sleep, clothing and transportation I need today. I come to Your throne for the discernment, words and empowerment I need to honor You and minister to the people You bring my way.

I turn away from fears and anxieties about the future. I do ask that You would prepare me for the future and prepare the future for me, but I also refuse to worry about either. Deliver me from every vestige of the fear of poverty and the love of money in my soul. I want to live for You and live in love here and now. This is the day that You have made; let me rejoice and be glad in it. Now is the day of salvation. Let not the past or the future rob me of the sacredness of this moment. In Jesus' name I pray. Amen.

Prayer for revelation of God's love

For this reason I bow my knees to the Father of our Lord Jesus Christ, from whom the whole family in heaven and earth is named, that He would grant you, according to the riches of His glory, to be strengthened with might through His Spirit in the inner man, that Christ may dwell in your hearts through faith; that you, being rooted and grounded in love, may be able to comprehend with all the saints what is the width and length and depth and height—to know the love of Christ which passes knowledge; that you may be filled with all the fullness of God.

Now to Him who is able to do exceedingly abundantly above all that we ask or think, according to the power that works in us, to Him be glory in the church by Christ Jesus to all generations, forever and ever. Amen.

—EPHESIANS 3:14–21

Prayer for boldness for spiritual leaders

Praying always with all prayer and supplication in the Spirit, being watchful to this end with all perseverance and supplication for all the saints—and for me, that utterance may be given to me, that I may open my mouth boldly to make known the mystery of the gospel, for which I am an ambassador in chains; that in it I may speak boldly, as I ought to speak.

—EPHESIANS 6:18–20

Prayer for love, faith and grace

Peace to the brethren, and love with faith, from God the Father and the Lord Jesus Christ. Grace be with all those who love our Lord Jesus Christ in sincerity. Amen.

—EPHESIANS 6:23–24

123

The Deer's Cry

I

I arise today
Through a mighty strength, the invocation of the Trinity,
Through belief in the threeness,
Through confession of the oneness
Of the Creator of Creation.

II

I arise today
Through the strength of Christ's birth with His baptism,
Through the strength of His crucifixion, with His burial,
Through the strength of His resurrection with His ascension,
Through the strength of His descent for the judgment of
　　Doom.

III

I arise today
Through the strength of the love of the cherubim,
In the obedience of angels,
In the service of archangels,
In the hope of the resurrection to meet with reward,
In the prayers of patriarchs,
In the prediction of prophets,
In the preaching of apostles,
In the faith of confessors,
In the innocence of holy virgins,
In the deeds of righteous men.

IV

I arise today
Through the strength of heaven,
Light of sun,
Radiance of moon,
Splendor of fire,

Speed of lightning,
Swiftness of wind,
Depth of sea,
Stability of earth,
Firmness of rock.

V

I arise today
Through God's strength to pilot me,
God's might to uphold me,
God's wisdom to guide me,
God's eye to look before me,
God's ear to hear me.
God's Word to speak to me,
God's hand to guard me,
God's way to lie before me,
God's shield to protect me,
God's host to save me,
From snares of devils,
From temptations of vices,
From every one who shall wish me ill,
Afar and anear,
Alone and in multitude.

VI

I summon today all these powers between me and those
    evils,
Against every cruel merciless power that may oppose my
    body and soul,
Against incantations of false prophets,
Against black laws of pagandom,
Against false laws of heretics,
Against craft of idolatry,
Against spells of witches and smiths and wizards,
Against every knowledge that corrupts man's body and soul.

VII

Christ to shield me today
Against poisoning, against burning,
Against drowning, against wounding,
So there come to me abundance of reward.
Christ with me, Christ before me, Christ behind me,
Christ in me, Christ beneath me, Christ above me,
Christ on my right, Christ on my left,
Christ when I lie down, Christ when I sit down, Christ
   when I arise,
Christ in the heart of everyone who thinks of me,
Christ in the mouth of everyone who speaks of me,
Christ in the eye of everyone that sees me,
Christ in every ear that hears me.

VIII

I arise today
Through a mighty strength, the invocation of the Trinity,
Through belief in the threeness,
Through confession of the oneness
Of the Creator of Creation.

Seven

"And Forgive Us Our Debts"

Prayer Element—Confession of Sin

Father of Life

I come before You fallen and weak
In search of Your mercy
Your unfailing love the drink which I seek
My spirit is thirstin'
Please remove my transgressions
Cleanse me from my sin

CHORUS
Father of Life please have mercy
Take this heart and give it purity
Father of Life pour Your mercy over me
And renew a steadfast spirit within me

Weathered and worn my life has been torn
My gaze has been drifting
I call Your name search me my Lord
My heart needs Your mending
Please remove my transgressions
Forgive me O God

(Repeat chorus)

BRIDGE
Receive my sacrifice
A broken spirit
Broken heart

In this phrase of the Lord's Prayer, Jesus Christ teaches us to seek forgiveness for our "debts." *Debts* are clearly a reference to our "sins"—the ways in which we "miss the moral mark" of our holy God's absolute standards of righteousness. This applies to our past—as well as our present—attitudes and behaviors. Jesus is safely assuming that we have failed and will fail again to hit the bull's-eye of God's target for our lives perfectly. This is why He instructs us all to seek God's forgiveness. The apostle James wrote, "We all stumble in many things" (James 3:2). It is in light of this that we need to confess our sins to our Father. Moreover, it is important that we do this continually throughout our lives.

As genuine believers, all of our sins are totally and forever forgiven once and for all through the power of the shed blood of Jesus Christ. Our relationship with God as our Father is secured by grace when we place our faith in Jesus' death for us. Yet in order to keep communication and fellowship with God flowing unhindered, it is vital that we humble ourselves by clearly acknowledging our failures when they occur. Such "confession is good for the soul" and helps to repel the pride, self-righteousness and self-deception that constantly and subtly seek to encroach upon and overtake us.

Many theologians have noted this difference between the "judicial" forgiveness that occurs when we are justified by faith in Christ's finished work and the "parental" forgiveness that is needed all along the way in our Christian experience. Once we are regenerated, God promises not to eternally judge or condemn us for our sins—past, present or future. He really becomes our Father and we His children. Bad behavior does not negate the family connection; it just warrants training and discipline. However, when we sin as Christians, we still need God's "parental" forgiveness, which keeps the warm relational channels open between us and our Father in heaven.

This prayer also is applicable to anyone who desires to

come to God and who is in need of asking for the "judicial" kind of forgiveness. God will graciously hear and answer the penitent cry of the sinner.

Two Opposite Extreme Views of Holiness

The enemy of our souls has used two different extreme theological views of sanctification (holiness) to keep believers from honestly confessing their sins. One view holds that believers have outgrown the possibility of sinning. The other view robs believers of the hope that they can actually live a life of substantial obedience to the words and ways of Christ. As a result, people who believe this view don't even make plans or entertain intentions to obey God. Both extremes have done great harm to many believers and to the witness of the church to the unbelieving, but watching, world.

In 1 John 2:1, the apostle says, "These things I write to you that you may not sin. And if anyone sins, we have an Advocate with the Father, Jesus Christ the righteous." John paints a picture of Christian experience that depicts sinning as an interruption to the norm for believers in Christ. The Holy Spirit empowers us to live above the "gravitational pull" of sin's power. However, if and when we do sin, or "stumble," as James puts it, we have a basis for receiving a fresh experience of forgiveness from our Father because of our trust in Christ. True believers are led by their changed hearts and by the prompting of the Holy Spirit's living within them to confess their sins to God so that the "relational air" stays clean between God and them. The blood of Christ sprinkled upon us and upon the mercy seat in heaven represents a valid and effective plea for our restoration to close fellowship with the Father.

Unconfessed sin doesn't instantly or automatically break our relationship with God as His children, but it certainly opens the door for spiritual problems—and other types of problems that flow from spiritual problems—to enter in and complicate our lives and relationships. If these problems remain covered up, they become cancerous to our life in the Spirit.

APOSTASY

Some Christians believe that apostasy (deliberately denying the essential doctrines and values of Christianity) can ultimately break a person's relationship with God as Father. Other Christians believe that such apostates were never genuine believers; therefore, the rejection of their once-professed faith is a sign that they never truly believed. They believe that a true Christian will never reject her or his faith. Either way, God does not give words of spiritual comfort to people who reject their faith in Christ. (See Hebrews 6:6–8; 10:26–27; 2 Peter 2:20–22.) God only gives sober warnings to people who are visibly identified with the Christian Church and who throw away their profession of faith. One thing is certain: Unconfessed sin has in fact built up in many human souls to the point of such apostasy. Sin is a serious thing—so serious that it required the death of the second Person of the Trinity to fully compensate for it.

CLEARING UP OFFENSES

Still, God is not shocked by any sin a person might commit—He knows well what we are capable of, and yet He loves us. Neither is God intimidated by the presence of sin in this world or in our lives. He only lovingly commands us to face our sins honestly, admit them to Him, ourselves and any other people who have suffered from them and sincerely verbalize our sorrow:

- "I'm sorry, Lord, for (the name of the sin)."

- "I'm sorry, (the name of the person), for (the name of the sin)."

It's really as simple as this—simply profound and profoundly simple. Our unwillingness to specify our failures usually betrays the presence of pride in our souls—the very root

133

of the spiritual problem that God requires us to confront. Many people want forgiveness from God without truly humbling themselves before His holiness and omniscience. God absolutely requires that our pride be broken, for He loves us too much to overlook it. Pride is a poison of the spirit that will spread to every arena of life if it is left unchecked.

We can all relate to this dynamic when we simply consider what we want from a loved one who sins against us—or perhaps what we *do not* want.

- We do not want some form of retribution.
- We do not want a half-hearted or reluctant apology for "hurting our feelings."
- We do not want escapist or blame-shifting admissions such as, "If I have offended you, please forgive me."
- We do not want our offender to *demand* that we forgive them: "Well, you *have* to forgive me because God says so."

Usually, we simply want a straightforward and humble acknowledgment of what they did against us (so that we know that they know!) and an expression of their hope and desire that we might forgive them. We want to see a spirit of truth and humility manifested in them.

Why is it often so hard for people to say these ten simple words: "I was wrong. I'm so sorry. Will you forgive me?" The answer is that many people are too steeped in pride to be that transparent with God and others.

THE IMPACT OF PAST HARSH DISCIPLINE

It seems that people who have been harshly disciplined and unjustly corrected by human authorities find it very difficult to "own" their failures straightforwardly. They are unable to feel bad about their offenses in a healthy way and to sincerely confess them. I believe that this is often because they were so shamed by these human authorities in an unjust and unforgiving way that they will do almost anything to avoid feeling any shame at all—even the right kind (Rom. 6:21). They rarely have the courage to take personal responsibility by facing the consequences of missing the mark and graciously receiving forgiveness from God and others in order to free their souls and restore their relationships to peace. Yet these are the very steps we need to take to cleanse our souls from sin and its effects. We must find grace to rise above the "victim mentality" that paralyzes us in our shame and keeps us from dealing with the presence of real sin and guilt in our own lives. No sin is too heinous for God to forgive—believing that it is is a misconception that keeps many people away from God and His people.

RECEIVING HEALTHY CORRECTION

In Hebrews 12:5, the writer quotes the proverb, "Do not regard lightly the discipline of the Lord, nor faint when you are reproved by Him" (NAS). This verse exposes two opposite, extreme and unhealthy human reactions to the correction that comes to us from God. The first is minimizing the correction by not paying proper attention to it. The second is overreacting to the correction and giving up trying to please God altogether. Rather than reacting in either extreme, God calls us to receive simply and humbly the correction that is for our training toward Christ-likeness. His discipline is actually proof that we are legitimate children of God, for He disciplines every true son and daughter. (See Hebrews 12:6–7.) God loves us so much that He accepts us just the way we are—but He loves us too much to leave us that way!

> **PRAYERFACT 13**
>
> —Prayerfact 12 (see page 118)
>
> *Original sin was a foreign invasion into what we were originally created to be and is also foreign to what we are destined by God to become. Sin doesn't seem so foreign and evil to us because we are so familiar with it.*
>
> —Prayerfact 14 (see page 136)

Instead of denying the truth that we sometimes sin, or capitulating to the idea that we can't help but sin, Jesus teaches us to pray, *"Forgive us our debts,"* when we do miss the mark. If we take this instruction to heart, not only will God forgive us, but we will learn to sin less and less as we interact deeply with our Father through Jesus Christ under the conviction and leading of the Holy Spirit. We will come to hate the sin that clouds our friendship with the Trinity and see it as the foolish and futile distraction and passion-draining thing that it is.

THE PRESENCE OF FORGIVENESS IN THIS WORLD

The Scriptures teach that we are not sinners because we commit sins—but that we commit sins because we are sinners. There is a systemic moral problem deep within our hearts that we inherited from our fallen forefathers. Sinners have begotten sinners (Rom. 5:12–19). The fact that we have consciously and willingly committed sins on many occasions, even violating our personal ethical codes, only confirms the point.

> ### PRAYERFACT 14
>
> —Prayerfact 13 (see page 135)
>
> *Only the power of God's Word and Spirit breaking in upon us from above can liberate us from our addiction to this independence and draw us into a glorious and noble dependency upon God's life. It doesn't come to us naturally, but supernaturally.*
>
> —Prayerfact 15 (see page 150)

Imagine how frightening it would be if there were no such thing as forgiveness from God! Many of us tend to take it for granted. Some people do not believe human beings need forgiveness from God, but even an honest brief glance into the human soul—or the daily newspaper for that matter— negates such a thought. We need forgiveness both for our "sins" and for our "sin."

Many people imagine that God forgives people because He is nice; however, this view denies the seriousness of sin—and the holiness of His character. God is holy, just and loving. His holiness and justice demand an accounting for sin, and His love compels Him somehow to make a way for this demand to be met effectively. He resolved the tension two thousand years ago by becoming human Himself, living a sinless life and bearing His own just wrath against the sins of all humanity. The second Person of the Trinity "became sin" (2 Cor. 5:21). He was beaten, and He bled and died on a cross that was designed for the execution of common criminals. Sin is so serious that "God in the flesh" was the only sacrifice worthy to remove its penalty and power. On the third day He was raised to life, never to die again, opening the way for forgiveness and a new life for any person who has the humility and courage to admit her or his need.

Enjoying Your Forgiveness

Some Christians have confessed their sins to God over and over again, and yet they never seem to get to a place of enjoying the forgiveness that God has promised to them. I have found that most people have two or three really "big" sins in their history for which they continually struggle to feel forgiven by God. It's easy for them to feel forgiven for many of their failures, but they seem to continue to punish themselves for those few most terrible things that they have done.

The best way to escape this spiritual trap is to realize that once we have sincerely confessed our sin—that thing for which we feel so guilty—to God, *it is a further sin not to receive the gift of forgiveness that God has promised to us!* This way of thinking takes our feelings out of the center of the situation and puts Jesus' feelings at the heart of the matter. Continuing to punish ourselves for our past confessed sins is like saying to Jesus, "I know that Your blood is precious enough to forgive me for all of those other bad things I have done, but it just isn't precious enough to forgive me for 'this one' and 'that one.' Sorry, Lord, I'll just have to keep beating myself up for these two." It's easy to see that this attitude is offensive to God and Christ when we put it in these terms. We are stubbornly refusing to receive the gift of God, and it hurts His heart in a terrible way.

Usually, when I have explained it this way to people, they find the courage and humility to confess the ongoing guilt of punishing themselves and see it for the foolish sin that it is. Then they are able to gain their spiritual footing and move significantly forward in Christ. If you have asked God to forgive you through Jesus Christ, please believe that you have received it, and then enjoy it—this honors God and glorifies His Son. If the devil comes back to remind you of your past sins, then respond by telling him you're glad that he just reminded you of how precious the blood of Jesus really is. He will change his tactics very quickly! Meditating on Psalms 32 and 51 is a great place to go to lead you through a time of confession after somehow failing to honor God.

1. Identify the classic sins into which you have fallen when you have gotten out of sync with the Holy Spirit. Commit the list to memory.

2. Ask God to give you a healthy view of receiving correction into your life and to heal your heart from any wounds of shame or indignity inflicted by past or present authority figures in your life. Express your trust in Him to correct you for your good.

3. Seek out a mature and trusted Christian of the same sex and confess to him or her the three most shameful things you have ever done. Ask the individual to pray for you and to proclaim God's forgiveness over you.

Father, if You would count iniquities, who could stand? But with You there is forgiveness. Father, I thank You for the sacrifice of Jesus—Your only begotten Son—on the cross.

Jesus, You endured the just wrath of Your Father against all the sins of all humanity from all ages. You who knew no sin were somehow made sin so that I could become the very righteousness of God in You. I had a debt I could not pay, and You paid a debt You did not owe.

I ask for a revelation from the Holy Spirit into the sinfulness of sin and for deeper insight into Your sufferings. I know that even now I have underestimated the priceless value of my salvation— for who can fully know its depths here and now? I humble myself again before You today. I welcome the searchlight of the Holy Spirit within my soul. I welcome You into the innermost chambers of my being where my motivations, attitudes and deepest beliefs are formed. In my innermost region, affirm what is right and check what is wrong. Please correct and redirect me from the inside out.

I welcome and need the convicting work of the Holy Spirit in an ongoing way in my life. Never let me take You and the great things You have done for me in Christ for granted, Father. I want to love and embrace Your discipline, for they are the way to real life. I thank You that You accepted me as You found me, but that You have loved me too much to leave me as You found me. I know that You have helped me to grow in Jesus, but help me to keep going in the right direction and never turn aside.

I will walk in the liberty You have won for me. O Jesus, Your blood is so precious, Your sacrifice was so great that my vilest offenses have truly been washed away. Thank You, Lord. You are so great and so kind. I pray in Your name. Amen.

Prayer for partnership in the gospel and Christian maturity

Always in every prayer of mine making request for you all with joy, for your fellowship in the gospel from the first day until now, being confident of this very thing, that He who has begun a good work in you will complete it until the day of Jesus Christ.

—PHILIPPIANS 1:4–6

Prayer for love, excellence and good fruit

And this I pray, that your love may abound still more and more in knowledge and all discernment, that you may approve the things that are excellent, that you may be sincere and without offense till the day of Christ, being filled with the fruits of righteousness which are by Jesus Christ, to the glory and praise of God.

—PHILIPPIANS 1:9–11

Prayer for knowledge and spiritual strength

For this reason we also, since the day we heard it, do not cease to pray for you, and to ask that you may be filled with the knowledge of His will in all wisdom and spiritual understanding; that you may walk worthy of the Lord, fully pleasing Him, being fruitful in every good work and increasing in the knowledge of God; strengthened with all might, according to His glorious power, for all patience and longsuffering with joy; giving thanks to the Father who has qualified us to be partakers of the inheritance of the saints in the light.

—COLOSSIANS 1:9–12

Prayer for encouragement and unity

For I want you to know what a great conflict I have for you and those in Laodicea, and for as many as have not seen my face in the flesh, that their hearts may be encouraged, being knit together in love, and attaining to all riches of the full assurance of understanding, to the knowledge of the mystery of God, both of the Father and of Christ, in whom are hidden all the treasures of wisdom and knowledge.

—COLOSSIANS 2:1–3

Eight

"As We Forgive Our Debtors"

Prayer Element—
Forgiveness of Others

ONLY YOU

You forgave those who caused You injustice
Even when they nailed Your hands to a tree
You left a pathway for Your friends to follow
Marked by the blood spilled for the whole world to see
There are some who have injured and harmed us
Willful intentions to hurt and offend
Oh but Your way is love Your way is righteous
So we extend mercy and refuse to condemn

CHORUS
Only You can give us our freedom
Only You can pardon from sin
Only You return the joy of salvation
We need the grace which comes only from You

We come before You broken and humble
Our hearts are heavy from the suffering we've caused
With shame we confess
Repent we have stumbled
Father forgive us
Redeem what was lost

(Repeat chorus)

We need the grace which comes only from You
Only You can free us

As we forgive our debtors." There are several astounding implications of Jesus' insertion of this little qualifying adverb *as* into the forgiveness equation. First, it implies that the righteous ground upon which we stand as we pray for forgiveness must be that *we* have first forgiven those who have offended *us*. Jesus made this clear when He said, "But if you do not forgive, neither will your Father who is in heaven forgive your transgressions" (Mark 11:26, NAS). Jesus is not saying that we earn God's forgiveness by the "good work" of forgiving others—we are saved by unmerited grace through personal faith in the Person and work of Jesus. Jesus is simply making a realistic observation. If our hearts are hardened and closed toward others, then they will be unable to be soft and open to receive freely God's forgiveness. A hardened heart is a hardened heart—whether hardened to others or to God! Our hearts must become soft and humble in order to receive Christ. Unforgiveness harbored in our hearts will bar the way for the love of God to enter in.

When we consider this objectively, we realize that it is rather hypocritical and inconsistent to ask God for mercy for ourselves while we are harboring resentment and bitterness in our hearts against others. "Blessed are the merciful, for they shall obtain mercy" (Matt. 5:7)—this is both a theological truth and a psychological observation! God loves us too much to allow us to go freely on our way in life when bitterness against others is firmly lodged in our hearts. Bitterness is a cancer that will destroy us and defile many others along the way (Heb. 12:15).

THE MINISTRY OF THE CROSS

The ministry of the cross of Jesus touches the deepest problems of the human spirit and condition. The work of Jesus Christ on the cross looms over all international human history as the most profound event ever. Its power is at work even to this day. The message of the cross ministers to the problem of real personal *guilt* in that *Christ died for us* on the cross.

> But God demonstrates His own love toward us, in that while we were still sinners, Christ died for us.
>
> —ROMANS 5:8

It ministers to the problem of our *powerlessness* to change ourselves into better people in that *we died with Christ* on the cross.

> Knowing this, that our old man was crucified with Him, that the body of sin might be done away with, that we should no longer be slaves of sin.
>
> —ROMANS 6:6

The cross also ministers to the paralyzing pain and power of *injustice* in that *Christ died*. The greatest injustice that the universe has ever known didn't happen to me or anyone else, but to Him. This is because He was and is God made flesh, the only truly innocent and sinless person to walk the earth since Adam and Eve fell in the garden. When God the Son was hanging on the cross, bleeding for the aggregate sins of all humanity, He appealed to God in prayer, "Father, forgive them, for they do not know what they do" (Luke 23:34). When we understand what His sacrifice means for each of us, the reality that Jesus did this will impart to us the courage we need to forgive those who have sinned against us.

> For consider Him who endured such hostility from sinners against Himself, lest you become weary and discouraged in your souls.
>
> —HEBREWS 12:3

THE UNJUST SLAVE

The passage in the Bible that is probably the most helpful to us in overcoming unforgiveness is the parable of the wicked servant (Matt. 18:21–35). This servant owed his master an astonishing sum of money. Yet when the servant appealed to his master for more time to pay his debt, the master all at once freely forgave him the whole debt. Who has ever heard of such a generous master? Are we not then shocked and outraged when we read how the servant immediately went forth and harshly demanded the repayment of such a small debt from his fellow servant? Are we not scandalized to learn that when his fellow couldn't pay, the wicked servant threatened to prosecute him to the fullest extent possible? Do we not cringe as we anticipate the end of the story when the master discovered what the wicked slave had done and reinstituted a precise justice in place of undeserved mercy?

VICTIMS AND AGENTS OF SIN

The point of the parable is that the power of heart it takes to forgive our debtors can only fully come when we do the following:

- View the injustices done against us in the light of the sins we ourselves have committed against God and His unparalleled holiness

- Consider deeply the unmerited forgiveness God offers us on the basis of Christ's sacrifice

The sins committed against us (we are all *victims* of sin to various degrees, and there is nothing we can do about this), no matter how vile, do indeed pale in comparison with our offenses toward God. We are also *agents* of sin (and we can do something about this).

Both the seriousness of our sinfulness and God's absolute holiness are impossible for us to comprehend or appreciate with our natural minds. Left to ourselves, we will minimize how offensive our sins are in the eyes of heaven. It takes a revelation from the Holy Spirit to impart such a perspective (John 16:8). However, God doesn't reveal to our hearts this awful truth in order to beat us down and wipe out our hope. On the contrary, He wants to bring us to the place of *reality* so that we can be led into the true liberation of our souls. The God who loves us knows, as no one else, how a spirit of unforgiveness will destroy *us*—our relationships and our very lives. God convicts us of sin for our good, not just for His or another's good.

DYING TO OUR DEMAND FOR JUSTICE

Forgiveness is absolutely essential to human life and to civilized society. Only forgiveness can reconcile man to God and man to man. Only forgiveness can put an end to the evils of racism, greed, selfishness and the vicious cycle of wars that proceed from such sins. Yet we all instinctively know that forgiveness is costly—never cheap or cowardly. Forgiveness takes a greater strength to give than any other gift that we can offer another. In fact, forgiveness requires a conscious sacrifice—a "death."

To grant forgiveness to another human, we must die to our demand for justice in this age. We must yield to God our perceived right to avenge ourselves, for He alone is capable of wisely dispensing vengeance at the proper time and in the proper way (Rom. 12:19). We must look upon the injustice without denying or minimizing its evil, and then put the matter of receiving personal justice into God's hands. This does not negate the need to perform our official roles in life as duly appointed authorities, such as being parents, church leaders or civil

---

PRAYERFACT 15

—Prayerfact 14 (see page 136)

God's liberation mission for our souls involves both crisis and process throughout the course of our lives as we are personally transformed and restored back into the image of God in us that was marred, although not eradicated, through the Fall of our first parents. Every crisis experience leads to further process; therefore, we should learn to be grateful for both crisis and process, the general ways that personal change occurs in us.

—Prayerfact 16 (see page 155)

---

authorities who must wisely discipline the guilty. These acts must be clearly distinguished from taking personal vengeance.

Forgiveness is a high and lofty virtue, and only the Spirit of God can give us the courage and power that offering it requires. Forgiveness is painful, but it opens the door to the love of God and neighbor and the joys that follow in its wake. It is important to remember that the availability of forgiveness from God also required a suffering sacrifice and death on His part. We must see the failures of other sinful and weak people toward us in contrast to our failures toward an infinitely perfect King. Just imagine, forgiveness cost God the most precious and valuable thing He possessed. It required the life of His only begotten Son and the loss of the unbroken love and bliss enjoyed between God the Father and God the Son from all eternity past to secure forgiveness for all humanity in such a way that God would not violate His justice or His holiness. Yet, we were worth it to Him! To reject the forgiveness God offers us in Christ is madness.

Only as we deeply contemplate the undeserved forgiveness our great Creator freely offers us can we find the emotional footing we need to forgive our debtors. We must press beyond the pain of our victimization by facing the guilt and shame that our significant evils against God and others have perpetrated, even though the degree of the evil usually isn't as obvious to us as to others. Why do we so easily see the injustices done against us without seeing the injustices we have done toward others? It is in light of this pain of conscience that we find the strength to forgive others. Then our hearts are set free to love.

THE DEMANDS BEHIND BITTERNESS

Some other things need to be said about forgiving others. Many times we do not experience a complete enough flushing out of bitterness from our hearts even though we attempt to verbalize forgiveness, to pray and to do loving things for those who have offended us in the past. This is confusing to us because we often feel that we have done everything we know to do to deal with the unforgiveness. The "catch" is that there is a deeper root problem that words, prayers and deeds do not necessarily touch. Beneath the bitterness problem there often is a pervasive hidden agenda, a selfish *demand* that no person will thwart our hopes and dreams for having good and pleasant life circumstances or a life free from the pain of injustice.

These unstated, but firmly entrenched, *demands* take on a driving energy within our souls to the point that they become the very *goals* for which we are living. The problem is, however, that if preferable circumstances become the goal of our lives, other people will have the ability to thwart them continually. This gives weak and fallen people far too much power over our lives and our souls—a power we must reclaim and then give to God alone. Only then will we no longer be tempted beyond our strength to wrongly control and manipulate others. When we are unable to achieve this impossible circumstantial goal of a pain-free existence, we become deeply angered and ultimately embittered against the people who have "sabotaged" our illegitimate demand. *Striving to forgive is futile as long as this wrong goal is still operative deeply within us.* The hidden goal must be displaced.

ADOPTING THE RIGHT GOAL

God never called us to adopt good and pleasant life circumstances as our primary goal for living. *The proper aim of every believer should be to become more and more like our Lord Jesus.* When this biblical goal is set within the depths of our souls, we begin to relate radically differently to people and circumstances that are beyond our control. We understand that our heavenly Father, as a master craftsman, actually uses the pain of rejection and injustice as a shaping tool to help sculpt and conform us into the image of Christ. Of course, He also provides the many blessings of goodness to help transform us into the image of His Son. This is how the apostle Paul could dare to say, "That I may know Him and the power of His resurrection, and the fellowship of His sufferings" (Phil. 3:10).

This is also the basis upon which James could say, "Count it all joy when you fall into various trials" (James 1:2). And again, why Paul could say, "I delight in weaknesses" (2 Cor 12:10, NIV).

Another way to state our goal of becoming more and more like Jesus is this: to get to know God better and better. It is primarily by the true and intimate knowledge of God that we are personally transformed.

> But we all, with unveiled face, beholding as in a mirror the glory of the Lord, are being transformed into the same image from glory to glory, just as by the Spirit of the Lord.
>
> —2 CORINTHIANS 3:18

Beholding is becoming! "They looked to Him and were radiant" (Ps. 34:5). We become like that upon which we worshipfully gaze. The longing to be personally perfected should override our lust for personal comfort and perfect justice in this life.

As we are philosophically and emotionally reconciled to the fact that our great and good Father will sometimes allow sufferings into our lives for our ultimate benefit, avoiding pain no longer remains the driving inner force of our lives. This change in emotional chemistry frees us truly and deeply to forgive people who have sinned against us. Then when people do offend us—and in this fallen world they always will—we experience *disappointment* toward them rather than *bitterness* against them. These two experiences are vastly different. Disappointment evaporates on the heels of prayers of forgiveness and acts of goodness, while bitterness is driven deeper into hiding as outward religious words and actions cover it up.

WHERE DO WE START?

One final thought on forgiving others needs to be considered. As we seek to have our spirits cleansed from unforgiveness, it is easy to become distracted by the painful, but minor, injustices done against us by people with whom we have had little to do. Most often though, forgiveness should focus on the *significant others* in our lives. These people usually have the most opportunities to sin against us. They are typically the ones who influence us most profoundly. Begin your search for hidden bitterness in reference to those relationships. The enemy would love for us to "leapfrog" over these primary relationships and focus on the people who have had less significant impact upon us. As odd as it may seem, deeply embedded anger toward a significant other may go undetected because we are skilled at gradually adjusting our style of relating to them so as to keep our anger toward them repressed. The ugly fruit of embedded anger will manifest itself in seemingly unrelated ways, and we can easily deny any suggested connection. We do this to cope with the pain of ongoing dysfunctional relationships with significant others in our lives. We are tempted to *blame* and *transfer* our negative feelings onto someone to whom we don't have a close attachment.

Ask the Holy Spirit to show you any people toward whom you have harbored bitterness, and He will be faithful, in His time, to show you. He loves to answer such "dangerous" prayers!

A VITAL DISTINCTION — UNCONDITIONAL AND CONDITIONAL FORGIVENESS

The devil has been able to keep many people in bondage to false guilt and confusion regarding forgiving others because of a lack of a simple, but absolutely vital, theological distinction. However, I have found that it is often overlooked and not generally understood by Christians. The Scriptures clearly teach a difference between *unconditional* and *conditional* forgiveness. These are two levels of forgiveness that have different ends to them.

> And whenever you stand praying, if you have anything against anyone, forgive him, that your Father in heaven may also forgive you your trespasses.
>
> —MARK 11:25

The forgiveness that Jesus speaks of here is comprehensive, unilateral and unconditional—*"anything* against *anyone."* This pretty well covers the bases. The goal of unconditional forgiveness is to *free our hearts* from bitterness and resentment so that we are able to "make room" in our souls for God's forgiveness toward us. This kind of forgiveness does not in any way refer to the condition or response of the person or people who have sinned against us. They may not even be aware that we are forgiving them.

The following verse relates to the second kind of forgiveness.

> Take heed to yourselves. If your brother sins against you,
> rebuke him; and if he repents, forgive him.
>
> —LUKE 17:3

The kind of forgiveness that Jesus now speaks of is different than unconditional forgiveness—*"if* he repents, forgive him." There is a condition attached to this level of forgiveness. In this case, forgiveness is a two-way street, and the goal of the interchange is a *relational reconciliation.* This is a deeper and most desirable level of forgiveness, but it takes both parties to achieve it. We cannot have reconciliation in relationship and the restored trust in the other person that flows out of it unless we are willing to confront them, if necessary, and they are willing to repent of their sin against us. This is why the apostle Paul wrote, "If it is possible, as much as depends on you, live peaceably with all men" (Rom. 12:18). Sadly, this is not always possible.

I have found that many believers "beat themselves up"

PRAYERFACT 16

—Prayerfact 15 (see page 150)

Christian maturity can be defined as vulnerable, responsible and strong dependency upon the Trinity.

—Prayerfact 17 (see page 168)

because they feel that God is asking them to trust people again who have grievously sinned against them, but who have never apologized or taken responsibility for the pain that they have inflicted upon them. These Christians assume that if they have really forgiven these people (who usually have at one time been very closely connected to them), then they should be able to relate to them as if nothing bad had happened between them. Yet their hearts are not free to really do this. So they wonder if God has really forgiven *them* because they are not "reconciled" to these people. They have never understood the distinction between unconditional and conditional forgiveness, and the enemy is using this to condemn them.

TRUSTING AGAIN

We are responsible before God to empty our hearts from resentment and bitterness, but we are not responsible to trust people absolutely who have sinned against us and never admitted to, apologized for and made amends for doing so. Neither are we responsible to somehow force people to repent for the wrongs that they have done. Unconditionally forgiving someone also does not imply that we pretend that the wrong never happened or that we do not feel pain over the wrongs done to us in the past. It does mean that we are not going to allow the pain of injustices to consume our lives and block us from walking with Jesus. It also means that we need to open our hearts to people who have sinned against us and who then take steps toward us for reconciliation. Jesus did say in connection with extending conditional forgiveness, "And if he [your brother] sins against you seven times in a day, and seven times in a day returns to you, saying, 'I repent,' you shall forgive him" (Luke 17:4).

Trust in a broken relationship is typically restored in stages. The first step is the openness of heart to desire its restoration. Then as both parties walk in the light, seek to understand one another and express love and kindness to each other, the bridge of trust can be rebuilt. Sometimes it is surprising how quickly this can happen. Time must be granted to the offended party on the part of the offender for this trust to be restored, and it should not be demanded. The repentant offender must stay vulnerable before God and trust Him to work in the heart of the one offended in the past. Depending on the nature of the past offenses, there will be other dynamics at work that factor into reconciliation. Each case will have unique features, but God will give the wisdom necessary to bring the healing if both parties are seeking His grace.

1. In an attitude of quiet prayer, ask God to remind you of the five most painful injustices in your past. Ask Him to show you any way in which you wrongly reacted to the pain you felt—a wrong vow you made, a lie you believed or a strength you overused to compensate for it.

2. Try to picture the faces of the people who have hurt you deeply in your life. Pray to God for each one of them to be led to Him to receive His forgiveness and blessing upon their life.

3. Picture Jesus on the cross, the sinless and fully divine Son of God, asking the Father to forgive those who were murdering Him. Ask God for the courage to forgive those who have sinned against you.

4. If you are preoccupied by the hurt you feel in a relationship with another believer, and that hurt is keeping you from enjoying fellowship with one another, consider going to that person with a humble spirit and telling him or her how you feel. Be open to hearing how you may have hurt that person also. Then pray together for a healing.

5. Read the story of Joseph in the last chapters of Genesis, and observe how he worked through the injustices done against him by his brothers.

Father in heaven, in the light of Your forgiveness toward me, I bring before You every person in my history and in my present circumstances who has offended me. Remind me of their faces. I have allowed them to have too much power over my soul. I have reacted to them instead of responding to You. I have wrongly and ineffectively protected myself instead of looking to You in my sufferings, and I have tried to handle this pain on my own instead of trusting You to work it for good. I have believed the lie that such pain is automatically counterproductive to my goal in life.

But You say that legitimate sufferings can serve to help me know You better. I have tried foolishly to cope with life by overusing my strengths, making unscriptural inner vows, making wrong demands and believing lies. Lord, deliver me from this mistrust in Your goodness. I believe in Your absolute goodness and reaffirm it to my soul today. I confess that You are the one who loves me perfectly, and I will not expect any fallen human to fill the place that only You deserve.

For these things I now receive Your forgiveness through Christ. Jesus, give me the courage now to forgive from my heart all who have done injustice toward me. I will forgive them—I do forgive them. I put their souls into Your capable hands. I sacrifice my "right" to perfect justice in this life. Help these people, Lord. If they don't know You, then bring them Your salvation. If they do know You, then I pray that they have repented for any evil that they have done to me or others. I will not hold any grudges toward these people. If they come and repent to me, I will seek to trust them again. Deliver me from any fears that keep me from passionately loving You and my neighbor. I pray in the strong name of Jesus. Amen.

Prayer for Christian maturity

Epaphras, who is one of you, a bondservant of Christ, greets you, always laboring fervently for you in prayers, that you may stand perfect and complete in all the will of God.

—COLOSSIANS 4:12

Prayer for faith, love and patience

We give thanks to God always for you all, making mention of you in our prayers, remembering without ceasing your work of faith, labor of love, and patience of hope in our Lord Jesus Christ in the sight of our God and Father.

—1 THESSALONIANS 1:2–3

Prayer for love and holiness

Now may our God and Father Himself, and our Lord Jesus Christ, direct our way to you. And may the Lord make you increase and abound in love to one another and to all, just as we do to you, so that He may establish your hearts blameless in holiness before our God and Father at the coming of our Lord Jesus Christ with all His saints.

—1 THESSALONIANS 3:11–13

Prayer for peace, holiness and spiritual protection

Now may the God of peace Himself sanctify you completely; and may your whole spirit, soul, and body be preserved blameless at the coming of our Lord Jesus Christ.

—1 THESSALONIANS 5:23

Prayer for the power and glory of God in Christian service

Therefore we also pray always for you that our God would count you worthy of this calling, and fulfill all the good pleasure of His goodness and the work of faith with power, that the name of our Lord Jesus Christ may be glorified in you, and you in Him, according to the grace of our God and the Lord Jesus Christ.

—2 THESSALONIANS 1:11–12

Nine

"And Lead Us Not Into Temptation"

Prayer Element—Guidance

Lead Me

You know when I rise up when I lie down
You know what my lips will speak
Before I say one single word
You know my deep thoughts
All that I treasure
You skillfully guide me
Make me know Your will

CHORUS
Father lead me
Away from the things of the world
Father lead me
By Your truth and light of Your word
Father lead me
Search my heart and lead me in Your way

If I go to the mountains
The depths of the oceans
It doesn't matter where I go
Your presence will be there with me
You knew me before birth
Laid out each moment
You've planned every day for me
Guide me in Your will

(Repeat chorus)

Isn't it fascinating that the guidance element of the Lord's Prayer relates specifically to the request to be guided *away from* temptation rather than to be guided *into* something good? The reason I say this is that many Christians are rather preoccupied with, grasping for and even nervous about discovering exactly where, when and what it is into which God wants to lead them. It is not necessarily wrong to ask God to guide us, but it at least needs to be noted that we should also be concerned about being guided away from negative things.

An important clarification should also be noted here at the start. Temptation literally means "to entice to sin." God never tempts us to sin, as James makes very clear.

> Let no one say when he is tempted, "I am tempted by God"; for God cannot be tempted by evil, nor does He Himself tempt anyone. But each one is tempted when he is drawn away by his own desires and enticed. Then, when desire has conceived, it gives birth to sin; and sin, when it is full-grown, brings forth death.
>
> —JAMES 1:13–15

Notice that James uses the phrase "He [God] Himself." This indicates a potentially confusing factor in the biblical teaching on temptation that must be directly addressed. The challenging point is that although God is never the direct agent of temptation, He, in His perfect wisdom, sometimes will allow us to be exposed to temptation that comes from a combination of internal (carnal desires) and external (demonic) enticements. God knows that a degree of exposure to temptation can, in the end, serve to strengthen our spiritual muscles via the resistance that we experience through it. We cannot become overcomers if we are never exposed to obstacles that we are called to confront and surmount.

As in the case of the temptation of Jesus in the wilderness, the Holy Spirit will sometimes lead us "into the wilderness to be tempted by the devil" (Matt. 4:1). If God had no redeeming use for the presence of evil in this world, He would have totally banished it long ago. It is out of the context of spiritual warfare that God is perfecting Christ's bride and preparing her for her destiny to rule and reign with Him in the ages to come. No one enjoys or looks forward to temptation. It is even offensive to consider that the evil one is sometimes permitted to communicate with us by putting thoughts in our minds and harassing us by manipulating people and circumstances. But temptation will be with us until the return of Jesus, and we must be reconciled to this harsh fact. The penalty of sin has been canceled by the work of Jesus on the cross, but the presence of evil in the earth has not yet been nullified.

Still, as the Lord's Prayer here indicates, we can pray for God to minimize our exposure to tempting situations. If we will so pray, I am convinced that we can learn many lessons directly from God without having to experience the oppression of temptations that force us into a learning posture. Many times we will have to learn through the "trial-and-error" method, but we can also learn without "trials" and "errors" if we stay intimate with God. We can fervently ask God, "Please teach me some other way, Lord. My ears are open, and my heart is teachable. Help me to obey quickly at the first hint of Your wisdom."

TEMPTATION VS. SIN

The inclusion of this phrase in the Lord's Prayer implies our need to admit frankly our susceptibility to being tempted. Overconfidence on this matter is ill advised. We need God's influence hourly to empower us to avoid situations that we know will be laced with temptations to sin. If it is not possible to avoid these situations, and often it is not, then we need God's influence to strengthen the resolve in our spirit to resist these temptations. There is a healthy sense of "not trusting ourselves" when it comes to the arena of temptation. Underestimating our capacity for carnality is extremely dangerous. The evil one has been at the game of temptations much longer than we have been at the game of resisting them or him. Both deserve a healthy kind of respect.

Temptation must be clearly distinguished from sin, for committing any specific sin is always avoidable. Crossing over the line of temptation into sinning occurs when the thought of compromising God's standard of righteousness is entertained, welcomed and pondered with the intent, or secret hope, to act it out. We sin when we *capitulate* to temptation. Jesus was tempted in all ways, and yet He never sinned (Heb. 4:15). While we cannot achieve perfection in this life, we can still avoid many opportunities to sin if we are prayerful and watchful. There is nothing noble about plunging headlong into circumstances that we know will hold temptations for us. "Discretion is the better part of valor," as the saying goes. God has clearly promised us that the Spirit will always provide a way by which we can *endure*, though not escape, any temptation that confronts us. However, we can always *escape* the specific sin into which any temptation is seeking to pull us (1 Cor. 10:13). Often this escape begins by simply fleeing the situation that is tempting to us.

As stated above, there are two main forces operative in any temptation. The first one is external, the second internal. The external force is Satan, also called "the tempter" (1 Thess. 3:5). He is not omnipresent as God is. He is a powerful, but finite and fallen, angelic spirit who was originally created by God. A third of the heavenly angels foolishly rebelled with him against God, and they were all banished from their dwelling place in the immediate presence of God (Jude 6). However, God did not immediately lock them completely out of His universe. Rather, for His own glory and fame, He decided to incorporate their evil presence and activity into the spiritual melodrama of His interaction with humanity and to prepare those human beings God would redeem for their appointed functions and purposes in the ages to come (1 Cor. 15:24–28).

HOW SATAN OPERATES

Satan tempts us first by manipulating the world system around us for his purposes. He influences human values, culture, laws, mores, traditions, customs, education, communications and governments. He also has a vast army of fallen angels—demons—who fearfully obey him as their master. These ranks of demonic beings are allowed to communicate to us personally. Demons can literally plant thoughts in our minds as well as manipulate and influence the people and circumstances around us. This is a nasty reality, but God has allowed it for our training and our ultimate good. Remember, our *resistance* to them builds spiritual *muscles*.

These forces of darkness actually study human beings and strategize ways to keep people from coming to Christ. If they fail at this, they specifically study believers and strategize ways to hinder them from serving Christ effectively. Believers are more specific targets of the evil one than unbelievers, for they are a much greater threat to his evil activity. In his book *The Screwtape Letters*, C. S. Lewis has given us masterful insight into how demons communicate and work together to tempt and deceive humanity into sinning.

Regarding the inward operative force in temptation, it is important to realize that our own imperfect minds and bodies can easily gravitate toward sinning, for these faculties are often used as conduits for the sin within us (Rom. 12:2). Especially on the heels of disappointment, we tend to look for false comforts in various kinds of sinful self-indulgence. Our bodily drives and passions are especially exploited, for they tend to assert dominance over our spiritual desires and therefore must

PRAYERFACT 17

—Prayerfact 16 (see page 155)

Life implies the presence of the power of an outward thrust of assimilating nutrients beyond itself. If we are to partake of God's life, then we must reach out and assimilate the things of the heavenly kingdom. This power is made available to us by God's gracious initiatives toward us.

—Prayerfact 18 (see page 171)

be "crucified" daily, along with any carnal attitudes and think-ing that may be working within us. These faculties must be put into their proper place of *subordination* to God's Word and God's Spirit. This means we must consciously rein in our med-itations and thoughts in order to align them with God's truth (2 Cor. 10:5). These human desires and powers are not evil in and of themselves, but there are biblical ethics that govern their proper place and use in our lives.

MORTIFICATION

The *sinful expressions* of our bodily desires and mental medi-tations must be denied and cut off altogether. This is the mean-ing of *mortification* in Scripture. (See Colossians 3:5.) Growing strong in the Spirit involves making the daily cruci-fixion of "the flesh" a habit. This is one primary way by which the intense demands of discipleship to Jesus can become an "easy yoke." With practice, following the commands and ways of Jesus can become second nature to us. Add to this the joy and delight of walking closely with God in the Holy Spirit, and we actually get "hooked on Jesus." Righteousness is the original "high" that our Creator has provided for our pleasure and delight. The highest possible pleasures and the deepest passions a human can know are found in rich experience with the living God. God has created our physical drives and desires for His glory and our enjoyment, but they are to be kept within the boundary lines divinely designated for their proper expression.

THE HABIT OF RIGHTEOUSNESS

When we face and overcome temptations to sin, we grow stronger in the Spirit of God. As we overcome many tempta-tions, yielding to the Holy Spirit's prompting and choosing acts of righteousness also become habitual. Obeying God therefore becomes easier and easier. When the Spirit led Jesus into the wilderness to be tempted by the devil, He faced essentially the same temptations that Adam and Eve faced in the Garden of

Eden. The lust of the eyes, the lust of the flesh and the boastful pride of life were the enticements used by the serpent to draw the first two humans into rebellion against God. Where our first parents failed, Jesus, armed with Scripture passages hidden in His heart, successfully resisted the devil's craft. The evil one even used Bible verses—though wrongly interpreted and applied—to tempt Jesus to sin. After passing this test, Jesus returned from the wilderness in the *power* of the Spirit and began His supernatural ministry (Luke 4:14).

THE FALSE SATISFACTION OF SIN

We must "keep [our] heart[s] with all diligence, for from it spring the issues of life" (Prov. 4:23). Temptation comes to us with a lie: "Give in to sin and you will be comforted and satisfied." Any sense of satisfaction, however, is temporary and false. Many people convince themselves, with the evil one's assistance, that sin is satisfying. This is the "deceitfulness of sin" at work (Heb. 3:13). It is the great allure of temptation. No one would sin if there weren't some form of pleasure associated with it. When sin becomes habitual, its power seems irresistible, even when the sense of satisfaction has long gone. Most people trapped in sin can't imagine themselves free from its grip. I believe this dynamic, perhaps more than any other, keeps people who have heard the gospel and intellectually know it to be true from accepting Christ as their Lord and Savior.

GETTING GUIDED

What could explain the strange absence of a request for being guided into *good things* (blessings) in the Lord's Prayer? Of course, there are Bible verses that do refer to this aspect of guidance. Yet here the Lord seems to emphasize that being guided into the blessings of God in life circumstances are a natural by-product of being good. "The steps of a good man are ordered by the LORD, and He delights in his way. Though he fall, he shall not be utterly cast down; for the LORD upholds him with His hand" (Ps. 37:23–24). The idea here is that we are to concentrate on "being good" rather than fretting and sweating about "getting guided."

Divine guidance is a promise from the Good Shepherd of our souls who longs, even more than we do, for us to walk in His will. Positive guidance begins with relational intimacy with God, not with getting ourselves into just the right specific circumstances or location. Guidance is first and foremost a matter of the condition of our inner being. We must remember that guidance is God's part. In essence, He says, "I know how to do it very well, thank you. You concentrate on delighting yourself in Me and My ways, and I'll take care of the rest. Trust Me, really!" Be good, in the true biblical sense, and you *will* be guided, for God has promised to do so. We need to focus on facing and surmounting the daily and hourly evil we face by loving God with all of our heart, soul, mind and strength and by loving our neighbor as ourselves.

Many elements of God's will are revealed in the teachings of Scripture. We cannot expect specific circumstantial guidance from

PRAYERFACT 18

—Prayerfact 17 (see page 168)

Now, in Christ and by the Spirit, we are empowered to respond to God's initiatives toward us, which will in turn set the stage for His responses to our response.

—Prayerfact 19 (see page 184)

God if we are not earnestly learning and applying the words of Scripture that already have given us clear moral guidance and wisdom for earthly life. Even when specific or special guidance does come to us from the Spirit of God, there are always many unknown elements regarding what should or will happen in the future. We "walk by faith, not by sight" (2 Cor. 5:7). Many Christians fantasize that God should constantly be showing them ahead of time what He's doing with them and what He will do with them next. Sometimes God does foretell the future by a "prophetic word," but Scripture and experience teach us that even more faith will be needed to obey Him if in fact He does give us prophetic direction. (See Isaiah 50:4–11.) For example, Abraham was told to leave Haran, which then required him to trust God for each new step as never before. There will always be uncertainties surrounding the details of the future in the normal Christian life. This dynamic keeps us walking step by step in dependency upon God.

SHOULD WE MAKE PLANS FOR OUR FUTURE?

It seems that in a way we can, yet in a way we can't, plan our lives and futures. This is a tension in life that God has deliberately set before us. If we knew too much about the details of the future, we would easily be distracted from loving God and the people around us. If we had no hints about our future, we would not be able to aim at accomplishing anything specific. But love, not planning out the details of our futures, validates our existence. Love is the overriding will of God for your life—right now, right where you are. Love *your* spouse, *your* boss, *your* children, *your* parents, *your* coworkers, *your* neighbors and *your* classmates, all in the name of God. And love them in the future also, whatever it holds and wherever you may be led.

If you are to find the will of God, you must find it in your current situation, for that is the only place where you are! Come honestly to God as you are. If you can improve your life, either morally or circumstantially, then make plans and efforts to do so. If improving your circumstances is beyond your control, then submit to the providence of God, and He will liberate your heart to find His will in your circumstances. If the Christian slaves referred to in the New Testament could be free in Christ, then it must be possible for us in our situations also (1 Cor. 7:21–23).

Most believers don't realize how effectively God is already guiding them. It isn't until we look back that we perceive how His invisible hand has indeed led us. If He has done it before, why fret that He has left His post? Love God and your neighbor, crucify your flesh daily, resist the devil and temptation, draw near to God and believe that He is guiding you, even though now His hand may be invisible!

1. Meditate on Psalm 139. Paraphrase it in writing and personalize it.

2. Do the same thing with Psalm 37.

3. List the seven most important people whom God has put in your life in this season. Make a plan to somehow express your love to them one by one in the next week.

Father, I thank You for the commitment You have made to me to be my teacher and guide. I put my confidence in Your ability to do these things more than in my ability to learn and follow. I do want to learn and follow, only I need Your help to be able. I know that evil is crouching at the door at every turn. You have said that I must rise up and master it. When it knocks, answer the door with me. Lead me away from all evil.

Your Word declares that You are able and willing to come to the aid of those who are tempted. I thank You, Jesus, that You subjected yourself to every temptation so that You can relate to the pressure to sin that I face each day. Please give me the wisdom to avoid many temptations. I will not walk close to the edge of the sheer face of sin's canyon. Yet, when necessary, help me to fight back every temptation that must come and find the way of escaping the sin behind the temptation that is seeking to rule over my soul. I know that I am capable and susceptible to the allure of sin. But by the work of Your cross my old self was crucified with You. May I reckon it so.

You have given me resurrection power by the Holy Spirit—may I choose this as my source of life every hour of each day. Reveal to me and remind me of the superior pleasures of walking in friendship with You. You hold the ways and words of life. I will trust You to lead me into the paths of righteousness for Your name's sake. Give me the integrity that will preserve me and guide me upon those paths. Amen.

Prayer for comfort and establishment

Now may our Lord Jesus Christ Himself, and our God and Father, who has loved us and given us everlasting consolation and good hope by grace, comfort your hearts and establish you in every good word and work.

—2 THESSALONIANS 2:16–17

Prayer for God's Word to be effective

Finally, brethren, pray for us, that the word of the Lord may run swiftly and be glorified, just as it is with you, and that we may be delivered from unreasonable and wicked men; for not all have faith. But the Lord is faithful, who will establish you and guard you from the evil one.

—2 THESSALONIANS 3:1–3

Prayer for love and patience

Now may the Lord direct your hearts into the love of God and into the patience of Christ.

—2 THESSALONIANS 3:5

Prayer for peace and nearness of God

Now may the Lord of peace Himself give you peace always in every way. The Lord be with you all.

—2 THESSALONIANS 3:16

Ten

"But Deliver Us From Evil"

Prayer Element—Warfare

Deliver Us

There's an enemy who stalks us
He is full of hate and lies
He is hungry to destroy us
To seize and end our lives
He's the ruler of darkness
Waiting for his prey
Son of David drive the evil one away

CHORUS
Deliver us arise arise O God
Deliver us from evil
Deliver us
Arise
Deliver us

He's a foe who's full of anger
Speaking doubt and causing fear
His intentions always evil
His motives always clear
He desires to take our freedom
Put on bondages of sin
Jesus Christ we pray deliver us from him

For still our ancient foe doth seek to work us woe; his craft and pow'r are great, and, armed with cruel hate, on earth is not his equal." These words are from Martin Luther's song "A Mighty Fortress Is Our God." They give us important insight now, as they have the church through the centuries. Humanity is engaged in a war with evil over which we have had no choice—we have been drafted into this battle! Behind all the impersonal evil in this world is a very personal evil. Satan is a real and invisible fallen archangel who is God's ancient adversary and our mortal enemy. He has significant power that should not be underestimated. Neither should it be overestimated.

The devil has been functioning as the god of this sinful age for a long time, and he is skilled at what he does. Left to ourselves, we are no match for him or his evil minions. However, the powers of heaven are available and accessible to us so that we can wage an effective war against him. God's power is unlimited, and Satan is ultimately no match for Him. God has allowed us to be engaged in this spiritual warfare in order to test, train and equip us for our destiny in the age to come—to rule and reign with Christ as the bride at His side for all eternity.

CHRIST'S TRIUMPH AND THE ONGOING WAR

Christ has already triumphed over all evil and the evil one through His finished work on the cross and by the power of His resurrection (Eph. 1:20–23; Col. 2:15). Paradoxically, however, the war is not over. Now God's people are called upon to arise in the power of Christ's resurrection and *also* to overcome the evil one, as Christ did (Eph. 6:10–20). We are called to participate in God's kingdom in partnership with our risen Lord on the basis of the spiritual authority He has purchased for us with His own blood and delegated to us by His Spirit. This honor is part of our inheritance in Christ (Ps. 149:6–9).

The spiritual battle with evil is an ugly reality; to deny this only leads us into further bondage to evil. Rather, we are called to engage courageously in the battle with wisdom and dignity. God wants to show Himself strong on behalf of those whose hearts are inclined toward Him. These are people who resolutely stand for the concerns of God and His kingdom regardless of the cost.

THE POWER OF AGREEING WITH GOD

We overcome the wicked one by "the blood of the Lamb and by the word of [our] testimony" and by not loving our lives "so much as to shrink from death" (Rev. 12:11, NIV). The fight is real and at times severe, but it is a "good fight" that we have been designed and equipped to wage (2 Tim. 4:7). We will know the joy of the Lord as we love what God loves and hate what God hates. His friends should be our friends, and His enemies our enemies. *Agreement with God* is the ground upon which we are called to stand and fight. This solidarity with God in spirit, word and deed is how we tap into and draw upon the powers of heaven as we are confronted with evil. "Greater is He who is in [us] than he who is in the world" (1 John 4:4, NAS). We are more than conquerors through Christ, and no matter what befalls us, we cannot be separated from His love for us (Rom. 8:38–39). We wage war for the sake of the love of God, and this makes it a holy and just war.

THE DEVIL'S CAMOUFLAGE

Satan and his demons would just as soon have humans believe that the supernatural demonic realm is a myth and that evil is merely an uneducated notion. The philosophy of *rationalism* has furthered this heresy in Western society over the past century and a half, granting the evil one all the more liberty to do his work without proper resistance from human beings. As a result, people become his unwitting pawns. The devil's primary methodology is to lure human beings (the flesh) and the systems and institutions they build (the world) into temptation and sin. When sin is mature, it brings forth death. Thus the devil, whom Jesus calls "a murderer from the beginning" in John 8:44, has his way in this fallen age. As long as the demonic realm can operate under the camouflage of the world and the flesh without allowing the supernatural source of evil to be exposed, the more effectively the devil is able to lull humanity into spiritual slumber.

The conjunction *but* in this phrase, "but deliver us from the evil one," vitally links this phrase with the previous one in the Lord's Prayer—"And do not lead us into temptation." The implication is that the main strategy Satan utilizes to accomplish his evil work is to tempt and entice human beings into sin. If he can trap us in sin, then he can effectively short-circuit either our relationship or our fellowship with the heavenly Father. He would rather work indirectly to get us to cooperate with him unawares, and have us mess up our friendship with God, than try to somehow get directly between God and us. Sin effectively separates and breaks down communication between humanity and a holy God. The devil is an ancient master deceiver who employs a multitude of tricks and a host of demonic underlings to imprison people in the ways of sin. He seeks to make sinning appear to be normal rather than subnormal, more pleasurable than righteous. Sin becomes cool, attractive, sophisticated, intelligent, necessary for survival, just and fair, a personal right, harmless, entertaining, unavoidable and—in the last resort—unpardonable. He dresses sin in any wrapping he can to keep people clinging to it.

THE SEVEN DEADLY SINS AND MODERN CULTURE

Theological and literary history have often referred to "the seven deadly sins." They are:

- Arrogance
- Envy
- Wrath
- Sloth
- Avarice (greed)
- Gluttony
- Lasciviousness (sexual lust)

PRAYERFACT 19

—Prayerfact 18 (see page 171)

Our response to God really matters and really counts—it is not a cruel game that the Infinite is playing with the finite.

—Prayerfact 20 (see page 187)

These seven deadly sins are alive and well in our world today. The apostle John boiled the essence of all the sin in the world down to the lust of the eyes, the lust of the flesh and the boastful pride of life (1 John 2:16)—covetousness, sexual lust and arrogance. The power brokers of modern society—media moguls, educators, entertainers, sports heroes, politicians and parents—have almost completely forgotten about the concept of sin. As a result, our society finds itself in a kind of moral schizophrenia.

We are shocked and outraged when young people calmly walk into their schools and shoot their classmates and teachers to death. Yet we don't make the obvious connection between this behavior and all of the gross and refined sins of parents and politicians, which we promote as socially acceptable.

The movie industry targets young (and older) people with an overwhelmingly powerful message that sex outside of marriage is fun, normal and unavoidable. Then we are scandalized by the sexual harassment going on in our schools and workplaces.

America devalued human life by legalizing abortion in the early seventies, yet we scratch our heads twenty-five years later at so-called mercy killings that treat the infirm and elderly as superfluous. Why should we be shocked if the logical end of this progression leads to "ethnic cleansing" and the martyrdom of Christians? These things are all philosophically connected. Some elite group independently determines who has forfeited their right to life.

Actually, what should shock us is that there are not more horrible events plaguing our society. Sadly, there will be unless there is a widespread spiritual revival of genuine Spirit-filled Christianity. Our nation needs a third great awakening to stem the powerful tide of evil and its social consequences. The day of judgment is swiftly approaching, and if our eyes are open, we can see that already the righteous judgments of God are being visited upon our culture. A friend of mine recently said, "There is going to be a *rude* awakening before there will be a *great* awakening." I believe it.

FREEDOM FROM SIN

There is a way out of sin. God can and will deliver us from the evil one and his snares. God invites us into the liberty of righteousness in Christ. He invites and gracefully entices us toward the superior pleasures of holiness: righteousness, peace and joy in the Holy Spirit. Through faith in Jesus Christ there is, first of all, forgiveness for the sins we have committed. This is a free gift that God offers us because Christ suffered God's wrath against all the sins of all humanity when He bled and died on the cross two thousand years ago. Secondly, God offers us a new life lived in partnership with the risen Christ, along with the gift of the Holy Spirit who gives us the power to live above the "gravitational pull" of sin. The Holy Spirit's living presence within us provides the "aerodynamics"— *forgiveness of sins* and *power over sinning.* Both of these things are freely offered to us by our heavenly Father if we will choose to believe in and follow His Son, Jesus, and thereby become His disciples—learners in His School of Life.

FIGHT OR BE CAPTURED

Earthly life, lived in this fallen world, is a constant war against evil and the evil one. Over this reality we have had no choice, even if we try to live in denial of it. We choose to fight through partnering with Jesus Christ, or we remain prisoners of war. Fortunately, there are also many blessings and joys God grants to us in the midst of the battles. These are the things that keep us encouraged so we can keep on fighting. *Every righteous belief, thought and action is an attack against the god of this world.* We need to broaden our understanding of spiritual warfare. We can, and must, adjust to living the life of a spiritual soldier.

There are aspects of our personalities that only become fully alive in the context of fighting against evil. Have you ever been strangely and deeply moved as you watched a powerful drama of good overcoming evil? Or have you ever felt a mysterious stirring within you, as if your hidden personal destiny was to engage in a noble war against the forces of darkness? This is God calling you to live as a friend of Christ. He lifts you up from the foolishness and boredom of sin into the blazing thrill and fascination of being intimate with the almighty God and serving His eternal purposes. We have not been created and placed on this planet to live a life of mere safety and self-protection. As we lay our lives down for Christ our King, we discover the real meaning of life. We are called to live a truly noble and heroic life, a life that is hidden with Christ in God. We are *personally engineered* by God to thrive as we are incorporated into a quality of life and purpose beyond our own, the very life and purpose of God our Creator, our great and good Father in heaven.

BELIEVE RIGHT, LIVE RIGHT AND FIGHT RIGHT

The Book of Ephesians is a wonderful treatise on how to prepare to engage and then how to actively engage in the spiritual warfare before us. It could be titled *Believe Right, Live Right and Fight Right.* Essentially the first three chapters deal with the basic doctrinal truths of Christianity. Chapters 4, 5 and the first part of chapter 6 exhort Christians concerning how to practically live in the light of God's truth. Starting in verse 10 of chapter 6 and going through the end of the book, it deals with the nature and strategy of our spiritual warfare. The order is not insignificant in our preparation to effectively face the evil that confronts us.

I have pictured this epistle like an arrow. The doctrinal section is represented by tail feathers, which give guidance and balance to the arrow in flight. Grand doctrinal truths that relate to the sovereignty of God, unmerited grace, the finished work of Jesus

Christ on the cross, the Person and work of the Holy Spirit, Christ's victory over all evil, personal redemption by faith, the nature of the universal Church and such are marvelously expounded by the apostle Paul. The practical living section is compared to the shaft of the arrow, which, if straight and true, is able to be sent effectively toward the intended target. Attitudes of the heart, meditations of the mind, use of the tongue, interpersonal relationships, time management (including the use of leisure time),

---

PRAYERFACT 20

—Prayerfact 19 (see page 184)

Our God is actually humble and condescends from outside and beyond time and space to enter into a genuine interactive relationship with us here and now in time and space. The true and living God is both transcendent and immanent. The deists (those who believe that God is uninvolved with His creation) cannot relate to His immanence, and the monists (those who believe that everything in creation is a part of God) cannot relate to His transcendence.

—Prayerfact 21 (see page 205)

---

marriage, family matters and vocational issues are all addressed from a profound and uniquely Christian perspective. The final section can be compared to the arrowhead, which can ably pierce and punish the spiritual enemies of God.

It is in these latter verses that Paul calls Christians to an effective defensive and offensive battle strategy against the invisible spiritual forces of Satan's kingdom. He uses the image of a Roman soldier's armor as a word picture of the powerful virtues and resources that God has made available to us to combat the cosmic echelons of evil powers ruling over this fallen age. Truth (including knowledge and integrity), righteousness, good news of God's peace terms, faith, right and hopeful thinking, the truth of the Scriptures, the Spirit's wisdom and powerful prayer—in all their various and creative forms and applications—are the elements that define the pieces of armor with which we are to outfit ourselves.

Your Kingdom Come

Christians are called to go on the *offense* to confront and overcome evil and all of its structures and manifestations in this world. However, we are not to go forth in a spirit of human anger and belligerence. "The wrath of man does not produce the righteousness of God" (James 1:20). The militancy of the body of Christ is not physical or carnal in nature:

> For the weapons of our warfare are not carnal but mighty in God for pulling down strongholds, casting down arguments and every high thing that exalts itself against the knowledge of God, bringing every thought into captivity to the obedience of Christ.
>
> —2 CORINTHIANS 10:4–5

Ours is primarily a fight for the hearts and minds of humanity. We are not to be intimidated by the false religions, philosophies and wicked ways of the world. We are called to humbly and boldly reach out to people in the name of Jesus Christ and simply hold forth His truth in love while living lifestyles that reflect His wisdom, kindness, sacrifice and beauty. We are not to be overcome by evil, but we are to overcome evil with good (Rom. 12:21).

Acknowledge the reality of the demonic realm, but don't "freak out" and be afraid of it. Rather, go forth and proclaim the Word of Christ in word and deed. Live daily for Jesus by practicing each of the following.

- Pursue the transcendent pleasures of God.
- Enjoy the God-given earthly pleasures of eating, sex within marriage, rest and the beauty of nature.
- Make sacrifices and deny yourself with rhythmic grace certain legitimate enjoyments in order to make more time and room in your soul for loving God and others.
- Read your Bible, and take it to heart.
- Worship passionately.

- Fellowship with other believers, and make them your closest companions.
- Share your faith with others.
- Engage in good works.
- Love and serve your family.
- Do your work as if God were your boss.
- Avoid vice and sexual sin.
- Pray hard.
- Play hard.
- Sleep well.
- Take care of your body.
- Listen to good music, and read good books.
- Listen to good preaching.
- Give to the poor.
- Help a pioneer missionary.
- Forgive your offenders.
- Confess your sins immediately.
- Be a faithful friend.
- Believe that God is near you in the mundane affairs of life.
- Sing loudly.
- Dance for God.
- Lay hands on the sick.
- Cast out demons.
- Listen well.
- Weep easily.
- Smile often.
- Hug and encourage someone.
- Don't gossip or slander others.

These are all acts of the holy war!

These ways of life, and others like them, will drive the devil away. When you meet him along the way, he will flee at your command, and you will destroy his evil works all around you. Be a powerful Christian for the praise and glory of Jesus and the Father.

1. Identify something in your culture or community that you know to be a manifestation of demonic deception or power. Ask God to expose this deception and reveal His truth and grace in its place.

2. Meditate on Ephesians 6:10–20. Think about how each of the virtues that are pictured as pieces of armor apply to the areas of life Paul identifies in chapters 4–6: your beliefs and thoughts, your speech, your interpersonal relationships in general, your sexuality, your time management, your entertainment habits, your marriage and family and your occupation.

3. Write down the specific lies that the devil has told you in the past. Renounce each one of them in the name of Jesus.

Dear Father, I will not hide my eyes from the awful reality of the presence of Satan and his angels in this world. Show me the evil behind the evils of this age. I want your ancient enemy to be my enemy as well. Strengthen me to put on the whole armor that You have provided for me—the belt of truth and integrity that frees my heart to run into the battle unhindered; the breastplate of righteousness that protects my heart against the allure and deceitfulness of sin; the shield of faith that causes my heart to agree with You, thereby quenching every lie of the evil one; the helmet of salvation that guards my mind and thoughts from any and all despair; the shoes of peace that help me go forth with grace to share Your great news with the lost; and the sword of the Spirit, which is Your living and written Word hidden in my heart and spoken from my lips that frustrates the enemy.

Deliver me from every plot and scheme of the adversary. I renounce Satan and all his works. Father, make me an overcomer who will lay hold of the fullness of my inheritance in Christ Jesus. Let everything I do be done in the name of Jesus Christ in such a way that You are glorified. May every word of my mouth and every meditation of my heart be considered an act of holy war against the evil of this age. I will not be overcome by evil, but I will overcome evil with good through the power of the Holy Spirit. Lord Jesus, through You I am more than a conqueror. Amen.

Prayer for all men and civil leaders

Therefore I exhort first of all that supplications, prayers, intercessions, and giving of thanks be made for all men, for kings and all who are in authority, that we may lead a quiet and peaceable life in all godliness and reverence. For this is good and acceptable in the sight of God our Savior, who desires all men to be saved and to come to the knowledge of the truth.

—1 TIMOTHY 2:1–4

Prayer for spiritual understanding

Consider what I say, and may the Lord give you understanding in all things.

—2 TIMOTHY 2:7

Prayer for spiritually deceived

And a servant of the Lord must not quarrel but be gentle to all, able to teach, patient, in humility correcting those who are in opposition, if God perhaps will grant them repentance, so that they may know the truth, and that they may come to their senses and escape the snare of the devil, having been taken captive by him to do his will.

—2 TIMOTHY 2:24–26

Prayer for effective sharing of the faith

I thank my God, making mention of you always in my prayers, hearing of your love and faith which you have toward the Lord Jesus and toward all the saints, that the sharing of your faith may become effective by the acknowledgment of every good thing which is in you in Christ Jesus.

—PHILEMON 4–6

Prayer for Christian maturity

Now may the God of peace who brought up our Lord

Jesus from the dead, that great Shepherd of the sheep, through the blood of the everlasting covenant, make you complete in every good work to do His will, working in you what is well pleasing in His sight, through Jesus Christ, to whom be glory forever and ever. Amen.

—HEBREWS 13:20–21

Secret Giving and Fasting: Keys to More Fervent Prayer

Take heed that you do not do your charitable deeds before men, to be seen by them. Otherwise you have no reward from your Father in heaven. Therefore, when you do a charitable deed, do not sound a trumpet before you as the hypocrites do in the synagogues and in the streets, that they may have glory from men. Assuredly, I say to you, they have their reward. But when you do a charitable deed, do not let your left hand know what your right hand is doing, that your charitable deed may be in secret; and your Father who sees in secret will Himself reward you openly.

And when you pray, you shall not be like the hypocrites. For they love to pray standing in the synagogues and on the corners of the streets, that they may be seen by men. Assuredly, I say to you, they have their reward. But you, when you pray, go into your room, and when you have shut your door, pray to your Father who is in the secret place; and your Father who sees in secret will reward you openly. And when you pray, do not use vain repetitions as the heathen do. For they think that they will be heard for their many words. Therefore do not be like them. For your Father knows the things you have need of before you ask Him. . . .

Moreover, when you fast, do not be like the hypocrites, with a sad countenance. For they disfigure their faces that they may appear to men to be fasting. Assuredly, I say to you, they have their reward. But you, when you fast, anoint your head and wash your face, so that you do not appear to men to be fasting, but to your Father who is in the secret place; and your Father who sees in secret will reward you openly.

Do not lay up for yourselves treasures on earth, where moth and rust destroy and where thieves break in and steal; but lay up for yourselves treasures in heaven, where neither moth nor rust destroys and where thieves do not break in and steal. For where your treasure is, there your heart will be also.

—MATTHEW 6:1–8, 16–21

Jesus' disciples must have marveled at the nature of His personal connection with the heavenly Father. Since solitude and prayer were a normal and habitual part of His lifestyle, the disciples must have seen Him steal away often to be alone with God. This was the source of Jesus' hidden life in the Spirit, a life that was fundamental to his public ministry. It is safe to assume that in the secret place of "watching and praying" Jesus prophetically "saw and heard" what His Father was "doing and saying" (John 8:28; 10:37). There He received His daily marching orders for entering into the good works that previously had been prepared for Him. Then, as now, an intimate life of communion with the Father was the key to success in both life and ministry.

It is also notable that Jesus is teaching us about prayer in the context of two other vital and fundamental disciplines for spiritual life in God's kingdom.

- Giving to the poor
- Fasting from food

These practices are to be engaged in "as unto the Lord." They are not merit badges of spirituality, flashed to impress people. On the contrary, Jesus teaches us that we should make deliberate efforts to hide the fact that we are engaging in these acts.

When Christians meet with frustration and despair in their efforts to dedicate themselves to prayer, perhaps they should take a look at these activities. Could it be that these disciplines are ingeniously designed by God to fuel one another rather than to be practiced independently of one another?

Since acceptable prayer is first of all a matter of having a right heart, it is helpful to consider the effect of fasting and giving on the human heart. Both Scripture and experience teach us that fasting humbles and tenderizes the heart before God. Hunger pains constantly remind us that we do not live by bread alone, but also by every word that proceeds from the mouth of God (Matt. 4:4). We more naturally look to God and are mindful of Him when we fast.

Giving to the needy *expands* the heart in compassion for people and connects us emotionally to the reality that we don't have the resources to provide for everyone in need. Only God does. Both of these heart-affecting exercises lead us back to the place of prayer because they serve to bring our very real dependency upon God to our consciousness. The God-fearing Cornelius was aware of this duo of pietous disciplines. His life of devotion before God's throne, even before his conversion to Jesus, opened the door for the good news of Jesus Christ to the whole Gentile world (Acts 10:1–4). If you have struggled to become the effective person of prayer you hope to be, consider adding secret giving and fasting to the equation.

Eleven

"For Thine Is the Kingdom, and the Power, and the Glory, For Ever. Amen"

Prayer Element—Bold Declaration

Hallelujah

You ride on a white horse
Scepter in hand
Lord You're a warrior
The holy Son of Man
Your eyes blaze like fire
Crowns upon Your head
You are the Word of God
The Beginning and the End

CHORUS
Hallelujah our Lord Almighty reigns
Jesus Christ our Savior reigns
Hallelujah Our Lord Almighty reigns
Our Lord our King our God

Son of the Highest faithful and true
Lion of Judah there is no one else like You
King of the Ages Bright and Morning Star
Wonderful Counselor
All of life is in Your charge

Behold the Lamb

Behold the Lamb of Glory
Light of the World
Your kingdom reigns forever
We worship You
(Repeat)

Holy Is the Lord

Every knee will soon bow down
And every tongue confess
That Jesus Christ is Lord
The Lion of the Tribe of Judah
The root of David is the King of kings
To Him who sits upon the throne
And unto the Lamb
Be blessing dominion and glory
And honor forever

CHORUS
And we cry holy holy holy is the Lord
Who was who is and who is to come

Only You are worthy to receive the power and the wisdom
   Lord
You're Captain and Commander
Master and Messiah Son of God
Let the redeemed bow down
And worship the Lamb
With blessing dominion glory
And honor forever

(Repeat chorus)

BRIDGE
Let us rejoice
Our God Almighty reigns
(Repeat)

(Repeat chorus)

The final phrase of the Lord's prayer is a bold prophetic declaration that helps set the direction of our hearts as we close the prayer and prepare to live our daily lives in this fallen world. The kingdom, the power and the glory belong to God forever. We declare it to God in praise. Let the angels hear it and rejoice. Let the demons hear it and tremble. Let the nations hear it and fall in line. Let our own souls hear it and be empowered.

The "for" links this decree to the former phrase, "and deliver us from the evil one." The Lord is God, and therefore the devil's claim to be god over the earth is merely smoke and mirrors.

SEEING THE KINGDOM OF GOD

When the devil tempted Jesus in the wilderness, he somehow flashed before Christ the kingdoms of the world, referring to his (that is, Satan's) power and their (the kingdoms') glory (Luke 4:5–8). However, Jesus knew that *the* kingdom and *the* power and *the* glory belonged only to His Father in heaven. He rebuked the devil and chose to worship and serve the One who alone is worthy of these things. Satan is a usurper and a liar, and we need to evaluate his resources and power in contrast with the one true God and His transcendent majesty. Christ is King of all the kings and Lord of all the lords. But He refused to take the demonic "shortcut" of accepting the inheritance of His kingship over the earth without enduring the suffering He had to face in order to overcome the evil in this world.

GOD'S OWNERSHIP OF CREATION

God has never abdicated His kingship over the earth. He has, however, purposely hidden it from the arrogant of heart. Jesus said that unless we are born from above, we cannot see the kingdom of God. It takes the quickening and revelation of the Holy Spirit to perceive God's loving, pervasive and gracious rule over the heavens and the earth. When our hearts are so awakened, we understand and see the signs and evidences that the whole earth is truly full of the glory of the Lord.

Camouflaged, yet right in the midst of the multitude of earthly kingdoms laden with sin, is the everlasting kingdom of God. Suspended above all the powers of this world that have been motivationally twisted by the pride of humanity is the almighty power of God. The radiant glory of God stands unmoved and untarnished behind the distracting and fading glories of this world. The meek receive the wisdom to know and touch these things. The humble rely upon these eternal and invisible realities to make their lives work. The wise repudiate dependence upon the substitute kingdoms, powers and glories that carnal people exalt.

BRAGGING ON OUR DAD

"Yours" stands out in relief not only against the backdrop of "theirs" but also "ours." "Not unto us, O LORD, not unto us, but to Your name give glory," said the psalmist (Ps. 115:1). As God blesses us by making His kingdom, power and glory accessible to us, we are tempted, as time goes by, to develop a wrong sense of "ownership" regarding these marvelous things. Overfamiliarity with holy things can cause the marvel of God and His kingdom to dim in our hearts. We are in need of the consistent spiritual renewal that softens our hearts and empowers us by the grace of God to remain in awe of God. Our heavenly Father is not only to be cherished by us, but He is also to be feared.

Little boys are famous for comparing among themselves the fearsome strength of their dads. Something godly is reflected in this natural dynamic. Children thrive on the awareness of their fathers' power and strength. There is something healthy about bragging about our dads. God grants us this one arena of legitimate boasting: "Let him who boasts boast in the Lord" (1 Cor. 1:31, NIV). This is because God has no false humility and therefore no qualms about encouraging us to glorify Him. He knows how glorious and extremely admirable He actually is, and He is a realist. He also knows how good it is for us to touch and be touched by His undeniable strength and majesty. God's desire for praise is not to boost a flagging and fragile ego, but to share with the whole creation the glory of His divine essence and power.

We always praise what is beautiful to us—a day, a song, a meal, a person. In essence, God says, "Delight yourself in Me, for I am delightful to the maximum degree, and I know it well. Praise Me to the extreme, for am I not the most beautiful Person in the universe? If you will, then I will let you feel My delight and share in the beauty and joy that is upon Me. If you stay real close, I'll rub off on you. Then we'll both be really happy."

PRAYERFACT 21

—Prayerfact 20 (see page 187)

The fundamental main means of our responsive communication with God has to do with prayer— talking and interacting with God who has chosen adapt His intentions and responses through this interaction with us.

CONCLUSION

So we have come to the end of the Lord's Prayer. We have meditated on some of the meanings of each phrase in the prayer with the idea in mind that each one contains many subtopics about which we speak to God. Each phrase of the prayer represents a movement in the larger composition. We have felt the various rhythms and moods within the spiritual music of the prayer—from the breathtaking awe of God's holiness to the passion of seeking to make His name famous in the earth. From the holy boldness and dignity of calling His kingdom and will to come to bear in our world to the sincere cry for our practical needs to be met each day. From the deep contrition of facing our own sins to the sweet release from the contempt and anger we have felt toward our offenders. From the hope of avoiding many temptations and trials to the nobility of facing our evil enemy and his schemes head-on. We then conclude with a confident expression of the ultimate victory that is God's alone.

Some times we may go through each of the movements of the prayer in one sitting or in one day. At other times, the Spirit of God may lead us to camp for days or weeks in just one of the movements. Ultimately, we will experience all of these spiritual rhythms as we walk on with God. May God add His blessing to you as you follow Him as He causes you live out the realities of this great prayer in all the various seasons of your life in Christ.

1. Take some time today to look past all the things that people have made that are all around you, and observe something that God Himself has created. Tell Him about the things you notice about it that seem marvelous to you.

2. Like Moses, ask God to show you His glory. (See Exodus 33:18.) Then look for it to manifest somehow.

3. Tell someone who doubts the reality or goodness of God that you have fallen in love with Him because you have perceived His beauty despite the fact that we live in a fallen age.

A Prayer from the Heart

Gracious Father in heaven, may my life more and more become centered in You. You are the Reason for all things. I proclaim Your goodness in the midst of many lying voices who insist You are not. You are the Victor, Lord Jesus. Already Your adversaries know it in their hearts. They are in panic, but You reign in unmoveable serenity and security upon Your throne. Put them to an open shame in the sight of all peoples.

To You alone I ascribe beauty, happiness, power, true love, justice, wisdom, strength, honor, riches, insight and foresight. You alone know me and love me nonetheless. You are the One I love. You are the One I live for. You are the One I will serve. I will not invest my strength in corruptible things, but I will seek today and forever to build my life on the unshakeable elements of Your unchanging personality and Your everlasting kingdom. Your child I gladly remain. Amen.

Prayer for healing

Confess your trespasses to one another, and pray for one another, that you may be healed. The effective, fervent prayer of a righteous man avails much. Elijah was a man with a nature like ours, and he prayed earnestly that it would not rain; and it did not rain on the land for three years and six months. And he prayed again, and the heaven gave rain, and the earth produced its fruit.

—JAMES 5:16–18

Prayer for maturity through sufferings

But may the God of all grace, who called us to His eternal glory by Christ Jesus, after you have suffered a while, perfect, establish, strengthen, and settle you. To Him be the glory and the dominion forever and ever. Amen.

—1 PETER 5:10–11

Prayer for prosperity

Beloved, I pray that you may prosper in all things and be in health, just as your soul prospers.

—3 JOHN 2

Prayer for stability and holiness

Now to Him who is able to keep you from stumbling, and to present you faultless before the presence of His glory with exceeding joy...

—JUDE 24

Prayer for the Second Coming of Jesus

He who testifies to these things says, "Surely I am coming quickly." Amen. Even so, come, Lord Jesus!

—REVELATION 22:20

Notes

CHAPTER 2
"WHICH ART IN HEAVEN"

1. Donald Guthrie, *New Testament Theology* (Downers Grove, IL: Intervarsity Press 1981), 874–888.
2. C. S. Lewis, *Miracles* (New York: Macmillan, 1960), 161.

PRAYING FOR ISRAEL
ACCORDING TO THE PATTERN PRAYER

1. This article is from the tract "Praying for Israel According to the Pattern Prayer" by David Harwood with Carl Kinbar, copyright © 1966. Used by permission.

You can experience more of God's grace & love!

*I*f you would like free information on how you can know God more deeply and experience His grace, love and power more fully in your life, simply write or e-mail us. We'll be delighted to send you information that will be a blessing to you.

To check out other titles from **Creation House** that will impact your life, be sure to visit your local Christian bookstore, or call this toll-free number:

1-800-599-5750

For free information from Creation House:

CREATION HOUSE
600 Rinehart Rd.
Lake Mary, FL 32746
www.creationhouse.com

Your Walk With God Can Be Even Deeper...

With *Charisma* magazine, you'll be informed and inspired by the features and stories about what the Holy Spirit is doing in the lives of believers today.

Each issue:

- Brings you exclusive world-wide reports to rejoice over.
- Keeps you informed on the latest news from a Christian perspective.
- Includes miracle-filled testimonies to build your faith.
- Gives you access to relevant teaching and exhortation from the most respected Christian leaders of our day.

Call 1-800-829-3346 for 3 FREE trial issues

Offer #AOACHB

If you like what you see, then pay the invoice of $22.97 (**saving over 51% off the cover price**) and receive 9 more issues (12 in all). Otherwise, write "cancel" on the invoice, return it, and owe nothing.

Experience the Power of Spirit-Led Living

Charisma
& CHRISTIAN LIFE

Charisma Offer #AOACHB
P.O. Box 420234
Palm Coast, Florida 32142-0234
www.charismamag.com